SUPPLEMENTARY GRAMMAR NOTES TO
AN INTRODUCTION TO MODERN JAPANESE
PART 1:   LESSONS 1-15

SUPPLEMENTARY GRAMMAR NOTES TO
AN INTRODUCTION TO MODERN JAPANESE
PART 1: LESSONS 1-15

Mutsuko Endo Simon

Ann Arbor

Center for Japanese Studies

The University of Michigan

1986

Copyright 1986

Center for Japanese Studies
108 Lane Hall
The University of Michigan
Ann Arbor, MI 48109

All rights reserved

ISBN: 0-939512-29-7

Library of Congress Catalog Card Number: 86-71897

Printed in the United States of America

CONTENTS

ACKNOWLEDGMENTS	viii
INTRODUCTION	ix
LIST OF ABBREVIATIONS	xi
HIRAGANA SYLLABARY CHART AND LIST OF THE KANJI USED	xii
LESSON 1: NEW VOCABULARY	1
LESSON 1: GRAMMAR	4

    I. X wa Y desu   II. X wa Y desu ka   III. X wa QW desu ka
    IV. Others

LESSON 2: NEW VOCABULARY	6
LESSON 2: GRAMMAR	9

    I. Ko-so-a-do Words   II. X wa QW desu ka   III. The Particles 'wa' and 'mo'   IV. I-Type Adjectives + Nouns
    V. ...o Kudasai

LESSON 3: NEW VOCABULARY	13
LESSON 3: GRAMMAR	15

    I. Particles   II. NOUN (X) no NOUN (Y)   III. Existence Constructions   IV. NOUN no LOCATIONAL NOUN
    V. SUBJECT wa LOCATION desu

LESSON 4: NEW VOCABULARY	20
LESSON 4: GRAMMAR	23

    I. Verbs   II. Verb Construction   III. Adverbs
    IV. More Examples of 'wa' and 'mo'

LESSON 5: NEW VOCABULARY	28
LESSON 5: GRAMMAR	32

    I. The Past Tense Form of Verbs   II. 'Yoku' (...AFF.) vs. 'Amari' (...NEG.)   III. Numbers and Counters   IV. QW + 'ka' vs. QW + 'mo'   V. Ko-so-a-do Words -- Out of Sight

| LESSON 6: | NEW VOCABULARY | 36 |
| LESSON 6: | GRAMMAR | 39 |

    I. Conjugation of i-Type Adjectives and the Copula
    II. CLAUSE (X) ga, CLAUSE (Y)   III. Negative Questions
    IV. Choice Questions   V. Numbers and Counters
    VI. Others

| LESSON 7: | NEW VOCABULARY | 44 |
| LESSON 7: | GRAMMAR | 48 |

    I. The -te Form of Verbs   II. VERB (STEM)-mashoo (ka)
    III. NOUN/ADJ-deshoo(ka)   IV. QW + 'de mo' (...AFF.)
    V. CLAUSE (X) kara, CLAUSE (Y)   VI. Numbers and Counters
    VII. 'Taihen' vs. 'Sukoshi'

| LESSON 8: | NEW VOCABULARY | 53 |
| LESSON 8: | GRAMMAR | 57 |

    I. VERB-te imasu   II. VERB (STEM) ni + Motion Verbs
    III. Particles 'de,' 'to' and 'ni'   IV. CLAUSE (X) no de,
    CLAUSE (Y)   V. Prefixes 'o-' and 'go-'   VI. The
    Particle 'mo'

| LESSON 9: | NEW VOCABULARY | 61 |
| LESSON 9: | GRAMMAR | 63 |

    I. The Plain Form   II. The Plain Form + to omoimasu
    III. The Plain Form + to itte imashita   IV. The Plain Form
    + deshoo   V. Noun Modification   VI. 'Moo' and 'Mada'

| LESSON 10: | NEW VOCABULARY | 68 |
| LESSON 10: | GRAMMAR | 71 |

    I. The Adverbial Form of i-Type Adjectives and the Copula
    II. The Plain Form in the Present and Past Tenses
    III. Noun Modification

| LESSON 11: | NEW VOCABULARY | 76 |
| LESSON 11: | GRAMMAR | 79 |

    I. A wa B ga C   II. Comparison Construction   III. VERB-ta/VERB-nai hoo ga ii desu   IV. The Plain Form + daroo to omoimasu   V. The Plain Form + 'kara' and 'no de'
    VI. Numbers and Counters

LESSON 12: NEW VOCABULARY	83
LESSON 12: GRAMMAR	86

    I. More Examples of 'A wa B ga C'   II. VERB-te kudasai-masen ka   III. CLAUSE (PLAIN) n(o) desu   IV. $VERB_1$ (STEM)-nagara $VERB_2$ V. CLAUSE (PLAIN) no   VI. CLAUSE (PLAIN) ka mo shiremasen   VII. '-mashita' vs. '-te imasu'

LESSON 13: NEW VOCABULARY	91
LESSON 13: GRAMMAR	94

    I. ADJ/VERB (STEM)-soo   II. VERB (PRES.) yotee desu   III. The Volitional Form of Verbs   IV. CLAUSE (X) keredomo, CLAUSE (Y)   V. The -te Form Indicating Reasons   VI. Time Clauses with 'toki' and 'aida'

LESSON 14: NEW VOCABULARY	100
LESSON 14: GRAMMAR	103

    I. VERB-te mo ii desu and VERB-te wa ikemasen   II. The Tense in 'toki'-Clauses   III. CLAUSE (X) ba, CLAUSE (Y)   IV. VERB (PRES.) hazu desu   V. DIRECT OBJECT (X) wa SUBJECT (Y) ga VERB   VI. The Particles 'made ni' and 'ni'

LESSON 15: NEW VOCABULARY	108
LESSON 15: GRAMMAR	111

    I. NOUN ga suki desu, VERB (DICT.) no ga suki desu   II. NOUN ga hoshii desu, NOUN o hoshi-gatte imasu   III. VERB (STEM)-tai desu, VERB (STEM)-ta-gatte imasu   IV. VERB (PAST, AFF.) koto ga arimasu   V. VERB (PRES.) tsumori desu   VI. '...na no de' vs. '...da kara'   VII. Polite Expressions   VIII. Some Notes on the Stems of Verbs

APPENDIX 1: SUMMARY OF PARTICLE USAGE	117
APPENDIX 2: LIST OF COUNTERS	121
JAPANESE-ENGLISH GLOSSARY	122
ENGLISH-JAPANESE GLOSSARY	129
INDEX TO THE GRAMMATICAL PATTERNS	137

ACKNOWLEDGMENTS

I would first like to express my appreciation to Professors Nobuko and Osamu Mizutani, authors of <u>An</u> <u>Introduction</u> <u>to</u> <u>Modern</u> <u>Japanese</u>, who graciously supported this project. This book is intended as a supplement to rather than a replacement of their textbook.

In the preparation of this book, I am in debt to many people, especially to Professor Shunichi Kato, without whose guidance, skillful assistance and encouragement this book would not have been possible; Professor Naomi Hanaoka McGloin, who introduced me to the art of writing grammar notes; Professor Akira Komai, who was instrumental in my undertaking this project; Professor Susumu Nagara, who gave me an opportunity; and to my students, whose valuable comments, suggestions and questions helped me immeasurably in the revision of the material.

I consider myself very fortunate to have such capable and hardworking research assistants, Robert Fouser, Lisa Murray, and, especially, Bruce McLennan, who carefully checked the material. Yoko Kato, who compiled most of the glossaries, has been an endless source of support and encouragement. It is impossible to express my gratefulness toward her.

This project was funded by the Center for Japanese Studies at the University of Michigan. My sincere appreciation goes to John Campbell, the Director, and Elsie Orb, Administrative Associate, for their continuous support over the years, and also to Bruce E. Willoughby, Associate Editor, for his editorial assistance.

Last, thanks to my husband Howard.

INTRODUCTION

This book contains notes on vocabulary and grammar to supplement An Introduction to Modern Japanese (hereafter IMJ). However, I have taken the liberty to include some additional vocabulary and grammatical items. I have also rearranged the order of appearance of some vocabulary and grammatical items to suit the needs and interests of students. This material has been tested and revised over several years while using IMJ at the University of Michigan and the Japanese Language School at Middlebury College. Although this book is designed to accompany IMJ, it can be used with many other textbooks and as a grammar book by itself.

Each lesson in this book is divided into two parts: New Vocabulary and Grammar. The new vocabulary is taken from the Dialogue, Explanation, Drills and Reading Comprehension sections of the corresponding lesson in IMJ. The added items are marked with an asterisk. In the first three lessons the vocabulary is presented in romanized script first and then in hiragana (and some in katakana). The same system of romanization is employed as is used in IMJ. (See pages vii-xi of IMJ.) However, devoiced vowels 'i' and 'u' are indicated as 'i̸' and 'u̸' in the romanized script in this book. Starting Lesson 4, only kana and some basic kanji are used. Almost all the kanji that appear in the first volume are accompanied by hiragana equivalents, although there will be less hiragana in the second volume.

The English gloss in the vocabulary section is kept brief. The main concern is to provide the primary meanings of the words and those that fit the context in the main text. Additional meanings are entered under "Rev." as they appear in later lessons. Some lessons, especially the earlier ones, introduce much vocabulary. The teacher might want to restrict the number of new vocabulary items the students are expected to be able to use actively.

It is very important to learn vocabulary in context. The short sample sentences, the translations of which are provided at the end of the vocabulary section, help students to be familiar with one of the typical sentences containing the vocabulary item and to learn the use of some particles, which often appear with it. When the subjects are not specified in Japanese, "I" or "he/she" is usually supplied in the English translation for the sake of convenience, although other subjects also may be possible.

An effort has also been made to keep the Grammar section concise. At the same time, the explanations are intended so that the students will be able to apply knowledge of grammar to other contexts beyond those presented in the text. Whenever possible, Japanese examples are given on the left side and the English equivalents on the right so that students can test themselves. It is hoped that students will practice reading Japanese sentences aloud many times. The goal is not really to "master" Japanese grammar but to be able to speak and understand the language correctly.

A summary of particle usage and a list of counters introduced in the text appear in the appendices. The words in the Japanese-English Glossary appear according to the Japanese "alphabetical" order. Study the hiragana syllabary chart presented on page xv. The glossaries can be used to find the English or Japanese equivalents of words and to see how they are written in kanji. For a fuller description and an example, consult the vocabulary section in the lesson, the number for which is indicated in the glossaries. These sections as well as the Index to the Grammatical Patterns should be useful in reviewing the material.

Good luck learning Japanese!

LIST OF ABBREVIATIONS

A, ADJ:	adjective
Ad, ADV:	adverb
Aff:	affirmative
cf:	compare
Conj:	conjunction
Cop:	copula
Dict:	dictionary form
Exp:	expression
Int:	interjection
Ir.V:	irregular verb
Lit:	literally
N:	noun
Neg:	negative
Opp:	opposite
P:	particle
PPhr:	particle phrase
Phr:	phrase
Pref:	prefix
Pren:	prenoun (words which can only appear as noun modifiers)
Pres:	present
Pron:	pronoun
QW:	question (interrogative) word
Rev:	review
Suf:	suffix
V:	verb
VN:	verbal noun
Vol:	volitional form

HIRAGANA SYLLABARY CHART

This is equivalent to the English alphabet. Memorize the order in which the syllables appear; <u>a</u>, <u>i</u>, <u>u</u>, <u>e</u>, <u>o</u>, <u>ka</u>, <u>ki</u>, <u>ku</u>, <u>ke</u>, <u>ko</u>, etc.

11	10	9	8	7	6	5	4	3	2	1	
N	w	r	y	m	h	n	t	s	k	VOWELS
ん	わ 　 　 　 を	ら り る れ ろ	や 　 ゆ 　 よ	ま み む め も	は ひ ふ へ ほ	な に ぬ ね の	た ち つ て と	さ し す せ そ	か き く け こ	あ い う え お	a i u e o

LIST OF THE KANJI INTRODUCED

LESSON 10: 十 二 月 九 日 一 七 田 中 人 日 本 四 年 三 千 円

LESSON 12: 来 下 白 大 金 私 今 行 子 語 時 前 何 言 分 山 川 上

LESSON 13: 読 話 食 学 入 週 六 休 良 買 先 午 八 見 早 雨 英 校

LESSON 14: 五 友 聞 方 毎 飲 間 生 車 安 書 思 火

LESSON 15: 売 会 高 国 文 手 紙 小 主

Lesson 1 (だいいっか): New Vocabulary
Dai ik-ka

Section 1:

	Romanized		English Equivalents	Hiragana	《 Katakana 》
*1.	watashi	【Pron】	I	わたし	
*2.	gakusee	【N】	student	がくせい	
*3.	sensee	【N】	teacher	せんせい	
*4.	Amerika	【N】	America	あめりか	《 アメリカ 》
*5.	Chuugoku	【N】	China	ちゅうごく	
*6.	Kankoku	【N】	Korea	かんこく	
*7.	Nihon	【N】	Japan	にほん	
*8.	Tanaka	【N】	Tanaka [SURNAME]	たなか	
*9.	Sumisu	【N】	Smith	すみす	《 スミス 》
10.	ee	【Int】	yes	ええ	
*11.	iie	【Int】	no	いいえ	
*12.	NAME-san さん	【Suf】	Mr./Mrs./Miss --; you	Tanaka-san たなかさん	
*13.	NAME-sensee せんせい	【Suf】	Prof.--; Mr./Ms.--; you (RE. teacher)	Tanaka-sensee たなかせんせい	
*14.	COUNTRY-jin じん	【Suf】	[NATIONALITY]	Chuugoku-jin ちゅうごくじん	
*15.	COUNTRY-go ご	【Suf】	[LANGUAGE]	Nihon-go にほんご	
16.	NOUN desu です	【Cop】	to be; am; is; are	Nihon-go desu. にほんごです。	
17.	NOUN wa は	【P】	[TOPIC]	Tanaka-san wa gakusee desu. たなかさんは がくせいです。	
18.	SENTENCE ka か	【P】	[QUESTION]	Tanaka-san wa gakusee desu ka. たなかさんは がくせいですか。	
19.	soo desu そうです	【Exp】	That is right.	Ee, soo desu. ええ、そうです。	
*20.	chigai-masu ちがいます	【Exp】	That is wrong. You are mistaken. [Lit. to be different]	Iie, chigaimasu. いいえ、ちがいます。	

Section 2:   Numbers and Time

(A) Numbers (Chinese Number Series)

1: ichi	いち	20: ni-juu	にじゅう
2: ni	に	21: ni-juu-ichi	にじゅういち
3: san	さん	30: san-juu	さんじゅう
4: shi/yon	し/よん	40: yon-juu	よんじゅう
5: go	ご	50: go-juu	ごじゅう
6: roku	ろく	60: roku-juu	ろくじゅう
7: shichi/nana	しち/なな	70: nana-juu	ななじゅう
8: hachi	はち	80: hachi-juu	はちじゅう
9: ku/kyuu	く/きゅう	90: kyuu-juu	きゅうじゅう
10: juu	じゅう	100: hyaku	ひゃく
11: juu-ichi	じゅういち		
12: juu-ni	じゅうに		
13: juu-san	じゅうさん		

(B) Time

1 o'clock: ichi-ji	いちじ	7 o'clock: shichi-ji	しちじ
2 o'clock: ni-ji	にじ	8 o'clock: hachi-ji	はちじ
3 o'clock: san-ji	さんじ	9 o'clock: <u>ku</u>-ji	くじ
4 o'clock: <u>yo</u>-ji	よじ	10 o'clock: juu-ji	じゅうじ
5 o'clock: go-ji	ごじ	11 o'clock: juu-ichi-ji	じゅういちじ
6 o'clock: roku-ji	ろくじ	12 o'clock: juu-ni-ji	じゅうにじ

Section 3:

21.	NUMBER-ji 　　じ	【Suf】	...o'clock	Ichi-ji desu. いちじです。
22.	(...ji)-han 　　じ　はん	【Suf】	half past...	Ichi-ji-han desu. いちじはんです。
23.	gozen ごぜん	【N,Ad】	a.m.	Gozen ichi-ji desu. ごぜん いちじです。
24.	gogo ごご	【N,Ad】	p.m.; afternoon	Gogo ichi-ji desu. ごご いちじです。
25.	ima いま	【N,Ad】	now	Ima gogo ichi-ji desu. いま ごご いちじです。
26.	asa あさ	【N,Ad】	morning	Ima asa desu. いま あさです。
27.	hiru ひる	【N,Ad】	daytime; noon	Ima hiru desu. いま ひるです。

28.	yoru 〖N,Ad〗 night; evening よる			Ima yoru desu. いま よるです。
29.	Tookyoo 〖N〗 Tokyo とうきょう			Tookyoo wa ima yoru desu. とうきょうは いま よるです。
30.	Nyuu Yooku 〖N〗 New York にゅーよーく 《ニューヨーク》			Nyuu Yooku wa ima asa desu. にゅーよーくは いま あさです。
31.	nan- 〖N〗 what [QW] なん			Nan-ji desu ka. なんじですか。
32.	Sumimasen. 〖Exp〗 "Excuse me." "I'm sorry."			すみません。
33.	Arigatoo gozaimasu. 〖Exp〗 "Thank you." (POLITE)			ありがとう ございます。
34.	Doo itashimashite. 〖Exp〗 "You're welcome."			どう いたしまして。

Classroom Expressions: The following expressions will be frequently used in class. You need not say them yet, but learn what they mean and respond appropriately.

a. Moo ichi-do (itte kudasai).　　　　　　　"(Please say it) one more time."
   もう いちど (いって ください)。

b. Minna de (itte kudasai).　　　　　　　　"(Please say it) together."
   みんなで (いって ください)。

c. Doozo.　　　　　　　　　　　　　　　　　"Please [go ahead]."
   どうぞ。

Translation of the Examples:

12. Mr. Tanaka; Ms. Tanaka
13. Prof. Tanaka
14. Chinese person/people
15. Japanese language
16. It's Japanese.
17. Mr./Ms. Tanaka is a student.
18. Is Mr./Ms. Tanaka a student?
19. Yes, he/she is.　[Lit. Yes, that's right.]
20. No, he/she isn't. [Lit. No, that's different.]
21. It is one o'clock.
22. It is one-thirty.
23. It is one a.m.
24. It is one p.m.
25. It is one p.m. now.
26. It is morning now.
27. It is daytime (OR noon) now.
28. It is night now.
29. It is night in Tokyo now.
30. It is morning in New York now.
31. What time is it?

Lesson 1: Grammar

I. X wa Y desu -- Statement meaning, "X is Y." "As for X, it is Y."

"X" is what you are talking about (i.e., the topic of a sentence), while "Y desu" is the comment (i.e., description) on that topic. The topic is usually deleted along with wa if it is obvious in a given context, as in the second sentences of Examples 2 and 3 below. Desu preceded by a noun is like the be-verb (e.g., is, am, are) in English. Remember that the verb always appears at the end of a sentence in Japanese.

	X		Y		
1.	Tanaka-san	wa	gakusee	desu.	"Mr./Ms. Tanaka is a student."
2.	Watashi	wa	Sumisu	desu.	"I am Smith."
			Amerika-jin	desu.	"(I) am an American."
3.	Tookyoo	wa	ima juu-ji	desu.	"(It) is 10 o'clock in Tokyo now." Lit. "As for Tokyo, (it) is..."
			Asa	desu.	"(It) is morning (there)."

II. X wa Y desu ka -- Question meaning, "Is X Y?" "As for X, is it Y?"

To change any kind of a statement into a question, just add ka at the end. (Do not use a question mark "?")

	X		Y		
1.	Tanaka-san	wa	gakusee	desu ka.	"Is Mr./Ms. Tanaka a student?" OR "Are (you) a student, Mr./Ms. T.?"
2.	Tookyoo	wa	ima asa	desu ka.	"Is (it) morning in Tokyo now?"
3.			Sumisu-san	desu ka.	"Are (you) Mr./Ms. Smith?"

Each of the questions above can be answered by "yes" or "no," as in Example 4 or 5.

4. Ee, soo desu.   "Yes, that's right." "Yes, he/she is." "Yes, I am."
5. Iie, chigaimasu.   "No, that's wrong." "No, he/she isn't." "No, I am not."

III. X wa QW desu ka -- Question with a question (or interrogative) word.

Questions asking "who, what, when, etc." must also have ka at the end.

	X			QW		
1.				Nan-ji	desu ka.	"What time is (it)?"
2.			Ima	nan-ji	desu ka.	"What time is (it) now?"
3.	Tookyoo	wa	ima	nan-ji	desu ka.	"What time is it in Tokyo now?"
	(Tookyoo	wa)	(ima)	juu-ji	desu.	"(It) is 10 o'clock (in Tokyo)(now)."

Questions 1-3 above cannot be answered by "yes" or "no"; you answer them by replacing the question word (nan-ji "what time" here) with the information called for (juu-ji "10 o'clock" in Example 3).

IV. Others

(1) Unlike English "Mr., Mrs., Miss --," --san in Japanese is never used for oneself. It is a suffix indicating POLITENESS and, therefore, is used only for others. It is rude, however, to use san to a teacher. When you address or refer to a teacher, you must say --sensee.

(2) There is no singular-plural difference for most nouns in Japanese. You interpret a certain noun to be singular or plural by the context.

(3) Wa and ka in X wa Y desu ka are classified as "particles." We will discuss what particles are in Lesson 3, so until then just learn how each of the particles is used.

Lesson 2 (だいにか): New Vocabulary
Dai ni-ka

1.	hon	【N】	book	ほん
*2.	jisho	【N】	dictionary [jibiki SOUNDS ARCHAIC]	じしょ
3.	pen	【N】	pen	ぺん 《ペン》
4.	enpitsu	【N】	pencil	えんぴつ
5.	tsukue	【N】	desk	つくえ
6.	isu	【N】	chair; stool	いす
7.	kasa	【N】	umbrella	かさ
8.	tokee	【N】	watch; clock	とけい
9.	kaban	【N】	bag; briefcase	かばん
*10.	kutsu	【N】	shoe(s)	くつ
11.	kutsu-shita	【N】	sock(s)	くつした
12.	nairon	【N】	nylon	ないろん 《ナイロン》
13.	momen	【N】	cotton	もめん
14.	mado	【N】	window	まど
15.	tatemono	【N】	building	たてもの
*16.	gakkoo	【N】	school	がっこう
*17.	toshokan	【N】	library	としょかん
18.	byooin	【N】	hospital; clinic	びょういん
19.	kore これ	【Pron】	this thing; these things [NEAR THE SPEAKER]	Kore wa hon desu. これは ほんです。
20.	sore それ	【Pron】	that thing; those things [NEAR THE LISTENER]	Sore wa hon desu. それは ほんです。
21.	are あれ	【Pron】	that thing; those things [FAR AWAY]	Are wa hon desu. あれは ほんです。
22.	dore どれ	【Pron】	which one/thing(s) [QW] [OUT OF THREE OR MORE]	Hon wa dore desu ka. ほんは どれですか。
23.	kono + NOUN この	【Pren】	this...; these... [NEAR THE SPEAKER]	Kono tatemono wa gakkoo desu. この たてものは がっこうです。
24.	sono + NOUN その	【Pren】	that...; those... [NEAR THE LISTENER]	Sono tatemono wa gakkoo desu. その たてものは がっこうです。
25.	ano + NOUN あの	【Pren】	that...; those... [FAR AWAY]	Ano tatemono wa gakkoo desu. あの たてものは がっこうです。
26.	dono + NOUN どの	【Pren】	which... [QW] [OUT OF THREE OR MORE]	Gakkoo wa dono tatemono desu ka. がっこうは どの たてものですか。

27.	akai あかい	【i-A】	red		Akai kasa desu. あかい かさです。
28.	shiroi しろい	【i-A】	white		Shiroi kasa desu. しろい かさです。
29.	kuroi くろい	【i-A】	black		Kuroi kasa desu. くろい かさです。
30.	aoi あおい	【i-A】	blue		Aoi kasa desu. あおい かさです。
31.	ikura いくら	【N,Ad】	how much (money) [QW]		Kore wa ikura desu ka. これは いくらですか。
32.	NUMBER-en えん	【Suf】	yen		Kore wa hyaku-en desu. これは ひゃくえんです。
33.	hai はい	【Int】	yes; yes, sir/ma'am [MORE FORMAL THAN ee]		A: Tanaka-san! B: Hai! たなかさん。　はい。
34.	aa ああ	【Int】	oh		Aa, soo desu ka. ああ、そうですか。
35.	NOUN + mo	【P】	also; too [SIMILARITY]	Kore wa jisho desu. Are mo jisho desu. これは じしょです。　あれも じしょです。	
36.	NOUN + o	【P】	[DIRECT OBJECT]		
37.	(NOUN + o) kudasai. を ください。	【Phr】	Please give me...		Hon o kudasai. ほんを ください。

Expressions:

a.	Ohayoo gozaimasu.	"Good morning." [POLITE]	おはようございます。
b.	Konnichi wa.	"Good afternoon." "Hello."	こんにちは。
c.	Konban wa.	"Good evening."	こんばんは。
d.	Sayoo nara.	"Good-bye."	さようなら。

Classroom Expressions:

e.	O-namae wa (nan desu ka).	"(What is) your name?"	おなまえは（なんですか）。
f.	Imi wa (nan desu ka).	"(What is) the meaning?"	いみは（なんですか）。
g.	Shukudai o dashite kudasai.	"Please turn in the homework."	しゅくだいを だして ください。
h.	Wakarimasu ka.	"Do you understand?"	わかりますか。
i.	Ii desu ka.	"Is it OK?" "Are you ready?"	いいですか。
j.	Yoku dekimashita.	"You did well."	よく できました。

Numbers:

100:	hyaku	ひゃく		1000:	sen	せん
200:	ni-hyaku	にひゃく		2000:	ni-sen	にせん
300:	san-<u>byaku</u>	さんびゃく		3000:	san-<u>zen</u>	さんぜん
400:	yon-hyaku	よんひゃく		4000:	yon-sen	よんせん
500:	go-hyaku	ごひゃく		5000:	go-sen	ごせん
600:	rop-<u>pyaku</u>	ろっぴゃく		6000:	rok<u>u</u>-sen	ろくせん
700:	nana-hyaku	ななひゃく		7000:	nana-sen	ななせん
800:	hap-<u>pyaku</u>	はっぴゃく		8000:	has-sen	はっせん
900:	kyuu-hyaku	きゅうひゃく		9000:	kyuu-sen	きゅうせん

Translation of the Examples:

19. This is a book.
20. That (near you) is a book.
21. That (far away) is a book.
22. Which (one) is the book?
23. This building is a school.
24. That building is a school.
25. That building (way) over there is a school.
26. Which building is the school?
27. It's a red umbrella.
28. It's a white umbrella.
29. It's a black umbrella.
30. It's a blue umbrella.
31. How much is this (OR are these)?
32. This is (OR These are) 100 yen.
33. A: Mr./Ms. Tanaka! B: Yes! (OR Here!)
34. Oh, is that right?
35. This is a dictionary. That too is a dictionary.
37. Please give me a/the book.

Lesson 2: Grammar

I. Ko-so-a-do Words

There are several groups of words in Japanese in which the words start with ko, so, a and do. We will learn two groups in this lesson.

When X (an object or a person) is either close to both the speaker and the listener or when it is closer to the speaker than to the listener, it is referred to as ko--. When X is closer to the listener than to the speaker, it is referred to as so--. When X is rather distant from both parties, it is referred to as a--. Question words in these groups all start with do.

```
                    a- ☂

                                    do- ?
           ko-  🚶 🚶  so-
              SPEAKER LISTENER
```

It is helpful to remember that "this/these" in English will always be ko--; "that/those" will be either so-- or a-- depending on the distance; and "which" will always be do-- in Japanese.

Kore, sore, are and dore are pronouns referring to things, and they cannot directly precede other nouns. Kono, sono, ano and dono, on the other hand, must be used before nouns. Therefore, it is incorrect to say: kore kasa, kono wa, kono desu, etc.

1. | Kore | wa | kasa | desu. "This (thing) is an umbrella."

2. | Kono kasa | wa | sen-en | desu. "This umbrella is 1,000 yen."

Examples 3-8 show some of the uses of these words. (All these questions can also be answered by simply saying: Ee, soo desu or Iie, chigaimasu.) One can mix kono..., sono..., ano... and dono... with kore, sore, are and dore in questions and answers, as shown in Examples 6-8.

3. Q: | Sore | wa | sen-en | desu ka.   "Is that near you 1,000 yen?"
   A1: Ee, |(kore| wa)| sen-en | desu.   "Yes, it (OR this) is 1,000 yen."
   A2: Iie,|(kore| wa)|ni-sen-en| desu.   "No, it (OR this) is 2,000 yen."

4. Q: | Are | wa | toshokan | desu ka.   "Is that over there a library?"
   A: Iie, |(are| wa)| byooin | desu.   "No, it (OR that) is a hospital."

5. Q: | Kore | wa | momen | desu ka.   "Is this cotton?"
   A1: Ee, (sore | wa) | momen | desu.   "Yes, it (OR that) is cotton."
   A2: Ee, (kore | wa) | momen | desu.   "Yes, it (OR this) is cotton."

6. Q: | Sono pen | wa | hyaku-en | desu ka. "Is that pen near you 100 yen?"
   A: Iie, (Kono pen | wa) | go-juu-en | desu. "No, it (OR this pen OR
        (OR kore | wa)   this) is 50 yen."

7. Q: | Ano tatemono | wa | gakkoo | desu ka. "Is that building a school?"
   A: Ee, (ano tatemono | wa) | gakkoo | desu.   "Yes, it (OR that building
        (OR are | wa)   OR that) is a school."

8. Q: | Kono kutsu | wa | go-sen-en | desu ka. "Are these shoes 5,000 yen?"
   A: Iie, (sono kutsu | wa) | yon-sen-en | desu. "No, they (OR those shoes OR
        (OR sore | wa)   those) are 4,000 yen."

II. X wa QW desu ka   cf. L.1, III.

It is important to remember where the question word appears in this type of question. Keep the same word order in your answer as in the question. Remember also that question words can NEVER appear before the particle wa (because you cannot say, for example, "As for which book, ..."). It is incorrect to say: dore wa, dono hon wa, etc.

```
              X            QW
1. Q:   | Tookyoo | wa | nan-ji  | desu ka.   "What time is it in Tokyo?"
   A:   | (Tookyoo | wa) | yo-ji | desu.      "It's four o'clock (in Tokyo)."

2. Q:   | Sore  | wa | nan   | desu ka.       "What is that near you?"
   A:   | (Kore | wa) | tokee | desu.         "It (OR This) is a watch."

3. Q:   | Kono hon | wa | ikura | desu ka.    "How much is this book?"
   A:   | (Sono hon | wa) | go-sen-en | desu. "It (OR That book OR That) is
        (OR  sore  | wa)                          5,000 yen."

4. Q:   | Jisho  | wa | dore | desu ka.       "Which (one) is the dictionary?"
   A:   | (Jisho | wa) | kore | desu.         "It (OR The dictionary) is
                                                  this one."

5. Q:   | Gakkoo  | wa | dono tatemono | desu ka. "Which building is the school?"
   A:   | (Gakkoo | wa) | kono tatemono | desu.   "It (OR The school) is this
                                                    building."
```

Now compare the following sentences:

6. | Ano tatemono | wa | byooin | desu.   "That building is a HOSPITAL."

7. | Byooin | wa | ano tatemono | desu.   "The hospital is THAT building."

- 10 -

You say Sentence 6 when you are talking about "that building." You and the other party see "that building," and you want to qualify or describe <u>what it is</u>. You say Sentence 7 when you are talking about "the hospital." The other party knows that there is a certain hospital, but he/she does not know <u>which one it is</u>. The questions which elicit these sentences will be 6-Q and 7-Q, respectively.

6-Q: | Ano tatemono | wa | nan | desu ka.   "What is that building?"

7-Q: | Byooin | wa | dono tatemono | desu ka.   "Which building is the hospital?"

You may not answer 6-Q with 7, nor can you answer 7-Q with 6. You must have the same "topic" (i.e., ...wa) in your answer as in the question. Simply put, you always talk about what the other party is asking about.

III. The Particles 'wa' and 'mo' -- CONTRAST AND SIMILARITY

We learned the particle <u>wa</u>, indicating the topic of a sentence, in Lesson 1. Another function of <u>wa</u> is to indicate "contrast." This is the opposite of the particle <u>mo</u>, which means "also; too." These particles are exclusive of each other, and they cannot appear together in a sequence.

1. | Watashi | wa | Amerika-jin | desu.   "I am an American."
   | Sumisu-san | mo | Amerika-jin | desu.   "Mr./Ms. Smith is also an American."

Note the use of <u>wa</u> and <u>mo</u> in situations such as the following:

2. A: | Kore | wa | nairon | desu ka. "Is this (made of) nylon?"
   B: Ee, | sore | wa | nairon | desu.   "Yes, that's nylon."
   A: | Are | mo | nairon | desu ka. "Is that over there nylon, too?"
   B: Ee, | are | mo | nairon | desu.   "Yes, that's nylon, too." [SIMILARITY]
   OR Iie, | are | wa | momen | desu.   "No, that's cotton." [CONTRAST]

IV. I-Type Adjectives + Nouns

There are two types of adjectives in Japanese, <u>i</u>-type and <u>na</u>-type. (We will study just the former type in this lesson.) An adjective, of either type, appears before a noun or a noun phrase which it modifies. <u>Kono</u>, <u>sono</u>, <u>ano</u> and <u>dono</u> would precede that whole phrase.

1. | Akai kasa | wa | san-zen-en | desu. "The red umbrella is 3,000 yen."
   | Kuroi kasa | mo | san-zen-en | desu. "The black umbrella is also 3,000 yen."

2. ‎ Toshokan ‎ wa ‎ ano shiroi tatemono ‎ desu.   "The library is that white
                                                     building over there."

V. ...o Kudasai   "Please give me..."   "I'll take... (IN A STORE)"

The particle o follows a noun and indicates the direct object of a verb. Kudasai is a verb in a special form which is used to request something politely.

NOUN
1. ‎ Enpitsu ‎ o kudasai.   "Please give me a/the pencil."

2. ‎ Sono aoi kutsu ‎ o kudasai.   "Please give me those blue shoes."

Lesson 3 (だいさんか): New Vocabulary
Dai san-ka

*1.	daigaku	【N】	university; college	だいがく	
*2.	kyooshítsu	【N】	classroom	きょうしつ	
3.	yuubinkyoku	【N】	post office	ゆうびんきょく	
4.	ginkoo	【N】	bank	ぎんこう	
5.	kíssaten	【N】	coffee shop	きっさてん	
6.	shokudoo	【N】	dining room; diner	しょくどう	
7.	hoteru	【N】	hotel	ほてる	《ホテル》
8.	robii	【N】	lobby	ろびー	《ロビー》
9.	erebeetaa	【N】	elevator	えれべーたー	《エレベーター》
10.	teeburu	【N】	table	てーぶる	《テーブル》
11.	koohii	【N】	coffee	こーひー	《コーヒー》
*12.	hako	【N】	box	はこ	
13.	chíkatetsu	【N】	subway	ちかてつ	
14.	to	【N】	door	と	
15.	hitó	【N】	person; people	ひと	
*16.	kodomo	【N】	child; children	こども	
17.	otoko	【N】	male (person)	おとこ	
18.	otoko no hitó	【N】	man	おとこの ひと	
19.	otoko no ko	【N】	boy	おとこの こ	
20.	onna	【N】	female (person)	おんな	
21.	onna no hitó	【N】	woman	おんなの ひと	
22.	onna no ko	【N】	girl	おんなの こ	
23.	go-shujin	【N】	(other's) husband	ごしゅじゅん	
24.	okúsan	【N】	(other's) wife	おくさん	
*25.	inu	【N】	dog	いぬ	
*26.	neko	【N】	cat	ねこ	
27.	Nakamura	【N】	Nakamura [SURNAME]	なかむら	

28.	ue	【N】	top; on; above	tsukue no ue	つくえの うえ
29.	shitá	【N】	bottom; under(neath); below	tsukue no shita	つくえの した
30.	naka	【N】	middle; inside; in	tsukue no naka	つくえの なか
31.	mae	【N】	front; before	tsukue no mae	つくえの まえ
32.	ushiro	【N】	back; behind; rear	tsukue no ushiro	つくえの うしろ
33.	tonari	【N】	next to; adjacent	gakkoo no tonari	がっこうの となり
34.	soba	【N】	near; close; by	gakkoo no soba	がっこうの そば
35.	yoko	【N】	side; beside	gakkoo no yoko	がっこうの よこ

36. koko	【N】	this place; here		ここ
37. soko	【N】	that place; there [NEAR THE LISTENER]		そこ
38. asoko	【N】	that place; over there [FAR AWAY]		あそこ
39. doko	【N】	which place; where [QW]		どこ
40. dare だれ	【N】	who [QW]	Ano hito wa dare desu ka. あの ひとは だれですか。	
41. nani なに	【N】	what [QW] [ORIGINAL FORM OF nan "what"]	Nani-go desu ka. なにごですか。	
42. NOUN-tachi たち	【Suf】	...and others; ...s [PLURAL, PEOPLE ONLY]	Watashi-tachi わたしたち	
43. arimasu あります	【u-V】	to exist; there is; have [THINGS ONLY]	Hon wa arimasu. ほんは あります。	
44. imasu います	【ru-V】	to exist; there is; have [PEOPLE AND ANIMALS ONLY]	Gakusee wa imasu. がくせいは います。	
45. NOUN ga が	【P】	SUBJECT	Gakusee ga imasu. がくせいが います。	
46. NOUN ni に	【P】	in; at; on [PLACE OF EXISTENCE]	Koko ni arimasu. ここに あります。	
47. X no Y の	【P】	X's Y; Y of X (X, Y = NOUN) [NOUN MODIFICATION]	Tanaka-san no hon desu. たなかさんの ほんです。	
48. SENTENCE ne ね	【P】	..., isn't it? ..., right? ..., you see? [TAG QUESTION]	Kore wa sen-en desu ne. これは せんえんですね。	
49. takusan たくさん	【N,Ad】	many; much; a lot	Hon ga takusan arimasu. ほんが たくさん あります。	

Translation of the Examples:

28. on (top of) the desk
29. under the desk
30. inside the desk
31. in front of the desk
32. behind the desk
33. next to the school
34. near the school
35. beside the school
40. Who is that person over there? (far away)?
41. What language is it?
42. we; us
43. The book is there.
    OR I have the book(s).
    [Lit. As for the the book(s), it (they) exists.]
44. The student is there. [Lit. As for the student, he/she exists.]
45. There is a student.
    OR I have a student(s).
46. It is here.
    [Lit. It/They exist(s) here.]
47. It is Mr./Ms. Tanaka's book.
48. This is 1,000 yen, isn't it?
49. There are many books.

Lesson 3: Grammar

I. Particles

"Particles" are attached to a noun, a phrase, a sentence, etc. They are usually short, and some have similar functions to those of prepositions in English (e.g., in, at, with). Particles, however, come after the elements to which they are attached.

(A) Types of Particles

Particles are classified into the following four types. The examples are taken from those introduced in Lessons 1-3.

(1) Grammatical Particles: ga (subject), o (direct object),
                             ni (place of existence), no (noun modification)
(2) Semantic Particles: wa (topic and contrast), mo (similarity)
(3) Sentence Particles: ka (question), ne (tag question)
(4) Conjunctive Particles: NO EXAMPLES SO FAR

Grammatical (or "case") particles are attached to nouns and indicate grammatical functions within a sentence, such as subject, direct object and indirect object. There are more particles of this type than of other types.

Semantic particles are attached to nouns and noun + grammatical particle combinations (and certain forms of verbs and adjectives). These particles do not change the grammatical functions but add additional meanings to the elements they follow. When combined with grammatical particles, semantic particles such as wa and mo replace ga and o, but co-occur with all others; e.g., X ni wa, and X ni mo, but not X o wa or X ga mo, etc.

Sentence particles appear at the end of sentences. The particle ne for tag questions is new in this lesson. Both types of questions are answered with "yes" or "no."

1. |Tanaka-san| wa |gakusee| desu ka.   "Is Mr. Tanaka a student?"
2. |Tanaka-san| wa |gakusee| desu ne.   "Mr. Tanaka is a student, isn't he?"

Conjunctive particles appear at the end of clauses. (A "clause" is a sentence within a sentence.) The functions of conjunctive particles are similar to those of conjunctions such as and, but, and because in English.

(B) The Particles 'ga' and 'wa' -- New vs. Old (or Shared) Information

The particle ga indicates the "subject" of a sentence. Since the subject is often the topic of the sentence at the same time and wa replaces ga in such a case, ga appears only in limited situations.

Use ga after a subject when you bring up the subject or an event anew. In the former case, X ga... expresses the meaning, "It is X who (or which) is/does ...," and hence, the subject (the element PRECEDING ga) becomes the main focus of the sentence.

The particle wa indicates the "topic" of a sentence. The topic may be the subject (which is often the case), direct object, location, or anything. The element preceding wa is something which has been mentioned or implied previously or something which can be surmised from the context. The element FOLLOWING wa becomes the focus of the sentence. This is why a question word can only appear after, not before, wa.

The kind of difference expressed by ga and wa is sometimes conveyed by the articles a and the and/or stress in English. Example 3 is a more common type of sentence than Example 4 in Japanese as well as in English, so use wa, rather than ga, after the subject in such sentences. (We will discuss the particles ga and wa in more detail later.)

3. Sumisu-san wa　Amerika-jin desu.　　"Mr. Smith is an AMERICAN."
4. Sumisu-san　ga　Amerika-jin desu.　　"Mr. SMITH is the American." OR
　　　　　　　　　　　　　　　　　　　　　"It is Mr. SMITH who is an American."

II. NOUN (X) no NOUN (Y)　　"X's Y; Y of X; etc." [NOUN MODIFICATION]

Modifiers always precede the words to be specified in Japanese. When X (a noun or a pronoun) modifies Y (another noun), X takes the particle no and precedes Y. The particle does not have a concrete specific meaning of its own, but simply indicates that the first noun modifies the second noun.

Since the last noun is the main noun, "X's Y; Y of X; Y at X" and so on in English will all be expressed with X first in Japanese. The phrase, X no Y (no Z...), as a whole is a noun phrase, and it functions as a noun within a sentence. Remember that the particle no cannot be used when an adjective or a verb modifies a noun.

1. Tanaka-san no kaban　　"Ms. Tanaka's bag" [OWNERSHIP]
2. onna no tokee　　"a woman's watch" [DESIGNED FOR WOMEN'S USE]
3. Nihon-jin no sensee　　"a Japanese teacher" [= The teacher is Japanese]
4. Tookyoo no tatemono　　"buildings in Tokyo" [LOCATION]
5. Kankoku-go no hon　　"a book written in or about the Korean language" [CONTENT]
6. Kore wa watashi no Nihon-go no sensee no kasa desu.
　　　"This is my Japanese (language) teacher's umbrella."

Note that proper nouns (i.e., names) usually do not take no; therefore, Examples 7 and 8 are quite different.

7. Tookyoo no daigaku   "a university (OR universities) in Tokyo."
8. Tookyoo Daigaku   "the University of Tokyo" [NAME]

III. Existence Constructions

The verbs meaning "to exist; to be (there)" are arimasu for things, and imasu for people and animals. The subject of the verbs may take either ga or wa depending on the context. A location phrase is marked by the particle ni. There are two types of sentences describing existence, as follows:

1. (A) Tookyoo ni daigaku ga arimasu.   "There are universities in Tokyo."

2. (B) Daigaku wa Tookyoo ni arimasu.   "The university is in Tokyo."

Do not change the word order or the particles (ga, wa, etc.) in the answer from what is in the question. Remember also that the questions containing arimasu and imasu may NOT be answered with "Ee, soo desu" or "Iie, chigaimasu." You must answer them by repeating the verbs.

We have a new set of ko-so-a-do words in this lesson: koko "this place," soko "that place near the listener," asoko "that place far away" and doko "which place." These are all nouns and, therefore, must be used with the particle ni in sentences ending with arimasu and imasu.

(A) LOCATION ni SUBJECT ga VERB "exist" [focus: WHAT/WHO is there]

3. Q: | Soko | ni | hon | ga | arimasu | ka. "Is there a book near you?"
   A: Ee, | (koko | ni | hon | ga) | arimasu. | "Yes, there is (a book here)."

4. Q: | Soko | ni | NANI | ga | arimasu | ka. "What is there near you?"
   A: | (Koko | ni) | hon | ga | arimasu. | "There is a book (here)."

5. Q: | Asoko | ni | kodomo| ga | imasu | ka. "Is there a child over there?"
   A: Ee, | (asoko | ni | kodomo| ga) | imasu. | "Yes, there is (a child there)."

6. Q: | Asoko | ni | DARE | ga | imasu | ka. "Who is over there?"
   A: | (Asoko | ni) | kodomo| ga | imasu. | "There is a child (over there)."

7. Q: | Koko | ni | neko | ga | imasu | ka. "Is there a cat here?"
   A: Ee, | (soko | ni | neko | ga) | imasu. | "Yes, there is (a cat there)."

8. Q: | Soko | ni | NANI | ga | imasu | ka. "What (animal) is there?"
   A: | (Koko | ni) | neko | ga | imasu. | "There is a cat (here)."

(B) SUBJECT wa LOCATION ni VERB "exist" [focus: WHERE something/someone is]

9. Q: | Hon | wa | koko | ni | arimasu | ka. "Is the book here?"
   A: Ee, | (hon | wa) | koko | ni | arimasu. "Yes, it is (here)."

10. Q: | Hon | wa | DOKO | ni | arimasu | ka. "Where is the book?"
    A: | (Hon | wa) | koko | ni | arimasu. "The book is here."

11. Q: | Kodomo | wa | asoko | ni | imasu | ka. "Is the child over there?"
    A: Ee, | (kodomo | wa) | asoko | ni | imasu. "Yes, he (OR the child) is over there."

12. Q: | Kodomo | wa | DOKO | ni | imasu | ka. "Where is the child?"
    A: | Kodomo | wa | asoko | ni | imasu. "He (OR the child) is over there."

13. Q: | Neko | wa | soko | ni | imasu | ka. "Is the cat over there?"
    A: Ee, | (neko | wa) | koko | ni | imasu. "Yes, she (OR the cat) is here."

14. Q: | Neko | wa | DOKO | ni | imasu | ka. "Where is the cat?"
    A: | (Neko | wa) | koko | ni | imasu. "She (OR the cat) is here."

Be careful not to confuse the "X <u>wa</u> Y <u>desu</u>" (Equational) construction with the Existence construction.

15. Q: | Dare | desu ka.   "Who is he?"
    A: | Tanaka-san | desu.   "He is Mr. Tanaka."

16. Q: | Dare | ga | imasu | ka. "Who is there?"
    A: | Tanaka-san | ga | imasu. "Mr. Tanaka is there."

IV. NOUN no LOCATIONAL NOUN

Locational nouns refer to locations relative to something (or someone). They are similar to words such as "top," "front" and "back," but there are also many which do not have equivalents in English. Noun <u>no</u> + locational noun forms a noun phrase and the particle <u>ni</u> is used after the whole phrase in sentences with <u>arimasu</u> and <u>imasu</u>.

1. hako no <u>ue</u>   "on (top of) the box; above the box"
2. hako no <u>shita</u>   "under the box; below the box"
3. hako no <u>naka</u>   "in the box; inside the box"
4. toshokan no <u>mae</u>   "in (the) front of the library"
5. toshokan no <u>ushiro</u>   "in (the) back of the library; behind the library"
6. toshokan no <u>soba</u>   "near the library; close to the library"
7. Sumisu-san no <u>tonari</u>   "next to Mr. Smith"
8. Sumisu-san no <u>yoko</u>   "next to Mr. Smith; beside Mr. Smith"

9. Q: | Kaban no naka | ni | nani | ga | arimasu | ka.   "What is in the bag?"
   A: | (Kaban no naka) | ni | jisho | ga | arimasu. | "There is a dictionary
                                                              (in the bag)."
10. Q: | Tanaka-san | wa | doko | ni | imasu | ka. "Where is Ms. Tanaka?"
    A: | (Tanaka-san | wa) | sensee no mae | ni | imasu. | "She (OR Ms. Tanaka) is in
                                                                front of the teacher."

Be careful of the word order in these phrases because they are the reverse of English equivalents. If you say locational nouns first, then the regular nouns appearing in the second position become the main noun.

11. a. tsukue no <u>ue</u>   "on (top of) the desk"
    b. <u>ue</u> no tsukue   "the desk at the top"

12. a. inu no <u>tonari</u>   "next to the dog"
    b. <u>tonari</u> no inu   "the dog next door"

To mean "in/at...," it is unnecessary (and sometimes inappropriate) to say ...<u>no naka ni</u> with nouns denoting places, such as <u>Tookyoo</u>, <u>toshokan</u>, and <u>kyooshitsu</u>, unless you want to emphasize the fact that something/someone is "inside." With this kind of noun, you can simply say ...<u>ni</u>.

13. Gakusee wa | kyooshitsu | ni imasu.   "The students are in the classroom."

<u>Tonari</u> and <u>yoko</u> are sometimes interchangeable, but <u>tonari</u> can only be used when you speak of two things belonging to the same category; e.g., one person next to another person, one building next to another. When you want to describe the location of a person next to a desk or a tree next to a building, and so on, you must use <u>yoko</u>.

V. SUBJECT wa LOCATION desu

Construction (B) above, "X <u>wa</u> Y <u>ni</u> imasu/arimasu," can be substituted for "X <u>wa</u> Y (location) <u>desu</u>" without changing the basic meaning of the sentence, but not Constuction (A). Since it is an abbreviated sentence, it sounds more abrupt and informal than "...<u>ni</u> imasu/arimasu" sentences. Remember that the particle <u>ni</u> is replaced along with the verb.

1. | Kasa | wa | koko | <u>desu</u>.
   = | Kasa | wa | koko | <u>ni arimasu</u>.

2. | Tanaka-san | wa | doko | <u>desu</u> ka.
   = | Tanaka-san | wa | doko | <u>ni imasu</u> ka.

3. | Neko | wa | isu no shita | <u>desu</u>.
   = | Neko | wa | isu no shita | <u>ni imasu</u>.

Lesson 4 (だいよんか):   New Vocabulary

1.	TIME に	【P】	at; on; in [SPECIFIC TIME]	いちじに
2.	PLACE へ	【P】	to [DIRECTION TOWARD]	がっこうへ
3.	PLACE で	【P】	at; in [PLACE OF ACTION]	がっこうで
Rev.	① (Xが) ある	【u-V】	to exist; (there) is; have X	ほんが あります。
	② (Xが) いる	【ru-V】	to exist; (there) is; have X (for X) to stay [ADDITIONAL MEANING]	こどもが います。
4.	(Xが) わかる	【u-V】	to understand X	にほんごが わかります。
5.	(Xが) はじまる	【u-V】	(for X) to begin; start	がっこうが はじまります。
6.	(Xが) おわる	【u-V】	(for X) to end; finish	がっこうが おわります。
7.	(Xへ) かえる	【u-V】	to return; go back (to X)	うちへ かえります。
8.	(Xへ) いく	【u-V】	to go (to X)	としょかんへ いきます。
9.	(Xを) よむ	【u-V】	to read X	ほんを よみます。
10.	(Xを) のむ	【u-V】	to drink X	コーヒーを のみます。
*11.	(Xを) たべる	【ru-V】	to eat X	ごはんを たべます。
12.	(Xを) みる	【ru-V】	to see; look at; watch X	えいがを みます。
13.	おきる	【ru-V】	to get up; wake up	しちじに おきます。
14.	ねる	【ru-V】	to sleep; go to bed	じゅういちじに ねます。
15.	(Xへ) くる	【Ir.V】	to come (to X)	ここへ きます。
16.	(Xを) する	【Ir.V】	to do X	なにを しますか。
17.	べんきょう	【VN】	studying; study	べんきょうを します。
18.	しごと	【VN】	work; job	しごとを します。
*19.	しつもん	【VN】	question	しつもんが あります。
20.	てんき	【N】	weather	いい てんきですね。
*21.	ごはん	【N】	meal; cooked rice	ごはんを たべます。
22.	みず	【N】	water	みずを のみます。
23.	おちゃ	【N】	tea	おちゃを のみます。
24.	テレビ	【N】	television	テレビを みます。
25.	えいが	【N】	movie	えいがを みます。
*26.	しんぶん	【N】	newspaper	しんぶんを よみます。
27.	ざっし	【N】	magazine	ざっしを よみます。
28.	うち	【N】	home; house [Lit. inside]	うちに います。
*29.	りょう	【N】	dormitory	りょうへ かえります。

30.	かいしゃ	【N】	company; office	かいしゃで しごとを します。
31.	えき	【N】	(train) station	えきへ いきます。
*32.	きょうかい	【N】	church	きょうかいへ いきます。
33.	やすみ	【N】	holiday; day off; vacation	やすみです。
34.	やました	【N】	Yamashita [SURNAME]	
35.	すずき	【N】	Suzuki [SURNAME]	
36.	～ようび	【Suf】	DAYS OF THE WEEK	
	にちようび	【N】	Sunday	
	げつようび	【N】	Monday	
	かようび	【N】	Tuesday	
	すいようび	【N】	Wednesday	use に
	もくようび	【N】	Thursday	
	きんようび	【N】	Friday	
	どようび	【N】	Saturday	
	なんようび	【N】	what day of the week [QW]	やすみは なんようびですか。
37.	すこし	【N,Ad】	a little; a few [Opp. takusan]	いすが すこし あります。
38.	きょう	【N,Ad】	today	きょうは げつようびです。
39.	あした	【N,Ad】	tomorrow	あした いきます。 no に
40.	こんばん	【N,Ad】	tonight	こんばん いきます。
41.	NOUNの あと	【N,Ad】	after...	そのあと、えいがの あと
42.	たいてい	【N,Ad】	usually; generally	たいてい ほんを よみます。
43.	ときどき	【Ad】	sometimes	ときどき ほんを よみます。
44.	すぐ	【Ad】	immediately; right away	そのあと すぐ かえります。
45.	まだ	【Ad】	still; (not) yet	まだ わかりません。
46.	もう	【Ad】	already; (not) any more	もう くじです。
47.	いい	【i-A】	good; nice; fine	いい てんきですね。
48.	いや（な）	【na-A】	unpleasant; nasty; disgusting	いやな てんきですね。
49.	はやい	【i-A】	early; fast	まだ はやいです。
50.	おそい	【i-A】	late	もう おそいです。
51.	まい～	【Pref】	every...	まいにち、まいあさ、まいばん
52.	お～	【Pref】	[POLITE]	おてんき、おちゃ、おなまえ
53.	TIME ごろ	【Suf】	around...; about...	にじごろ(に) いきます。
54.	あ OR あっ	【Int】	[SUDDEN REALIZATION]	あ、もう えきですね。

Expressions:

- a. おやすみなさい。 "Good night."
- b. しつれいします。 "Please excuse me." Lit. "I'll lose courtesy."
  ALSO, A POLITE WAY OF SAYING "Good-bye" TO SOMEONE OLDER THAN YOU OR HIGHER IN RANK

Translation of the Examples:

Rev. ① There is a book.
OR I have a book.
② There is a child.
OR I have a child.
OR The child stays.
1. at one o'clock.
2. to school
3. at school
4. I understand Japanese.
5. The school starts.
6. The school ends.
7. I return (OR go) home.
8. I go to the library.
9. I read books.
10. I drink coffee.
11. I eat meals.
12. I see movies.
13. I get up at seven o'clock.
14. I go to bed at eleven o'clock.
15. I come here.
16. What do/will you do?
17. I study.
18. I work.
19. I have a question.
20. Nice weather, isn't it?
OR The sun is out, isn't it?
21. I eat (meals).
22. I drink water.
23. I drink tea.
24. I watch television.
25. I see movies.
26. I read the newspaper.
27. I read magazines.
28. I stay at home.
29. I go back to the dormitory.
30. I work in the office (Lit. company).
31. I go to the station.
32. I go to church.
33. It's a holiday.
36. What day of the week is your day off?
37. There are a few chairs.
38. Today is Monday.
39. I will go tomorrow.
40. I will go tonight.
41. after that, after the movie
42. I usually read books.
43. I sometimes read books.
44. I go back right after that.
45. I don't know yet.
OR I still don't know.
46. It's already nine o'clock.
47. Nice weather, isn't it?
OR The sun is out, isn't it?
48. Nasty weather, isn't it?
49. It's still early.
50. It's already late.
51. every day, every morning, every night
52. POLITE WAY OF SAYING -- weather, tea, name
53. I will go around two o'clock.
54. Oh, it's already the station, isn't it?

Lesson 4: Grammar

I. Verbs

Two types of basic sentence structures were introduced in the previous lessons. In this lesson, we will learn the third type which involves various verbs.

1. X wa (OR ga) Y desu.   [EQUATIONAL CONSTRUCTION]
2. X wa Y ni (OR Y ni X ga) arimasu/imasu.   [EXISTENCE CONSTRUCTION]
3. X wa (OR ga) VERB.   [VERB CONSTRUCTION]

All Japanese verbs exhibit one or the other feature of the following sets:

(1) Present/Future or Past Tense
(2) Affirmative or Negative
(3) Plain or Polite Style

The most basic form of a verb is the present/future tense, affirmative, plain form, and it is called the "dictionary" form. To find a verb in a dictionary, you must look it up under this form.

Japanese is characterized by various speech levels which show familiarity or distance between the speaker and the listener. At the end of sentences the "plain" form is used in familiar speech, while the "polite" form is used in polite speech. For now, we will deal with only the polite (-desu/-masu) form.

There is no distinction between the present and future tenses; it is determined from the context. For example, the dictionary form of "to go," iku, and its polite counterpart, ikimasu, mean either "someone goes" (habitual action) or "someone will go" (future action). We will hereafter refer to the future/present tense simply as "present" for convenience. (We will learn the past tense form in Lesson 5.)

(A) Groups of Verbs

Verbs are classified into three major groups according to their dictionary forms: u-verbs, ru-verbs and irregular verbs. The grouping is purely based on the form and has nothing to do with the meanings of verbs. Each group has its own conjugation.

　　u-verbs:　All verbs which are neither ru- nor irregular verbs.
　　　　　　　aru, wakaru, hajimaru, owaru, kaeru, iku, yomu, nomu

　　ru-verbs:　Verbs which end in either -iru or -eru.
　　　　　　　iru, okiru, miru, taberu, neru　[EXCEPTION: kaeru is an u-verb]

Irregular verbs: kuru "to come" and suru "to do" only.

(B) The Dictionary Form ⇨ the Polite (-masu) Form

u-verbs: Drop -u at the end of the dictionary form and add -i-masu.
iku → iki-masu, yomu → yomi-masu, kaeru → kaeri-masu

ru-verbs: Drop -ru at the end of the dictionary form and add -masu.
miru → mi-masu, okiru → oki-masu, taberu → tabe-masu

Irregular verbs: kuru → ki-masu, suru → shi-masu

(C) Affirmative ⇨ Negative (in the Polite Form)

All verbs: -masu "does/will do..." ⇨ -masen "does/will not do..."
nomi-masu → nomi-masen, ne-masu → ne-masen, ki-masu → ki-masen

II. Verb Construction

(A) The New Particles 'ni,' 'e' and 'de'

A time word + ni indicates a specific "point in time." It corresponds to "in; at; on" in English in such phrases as "in April; at six o'clock; on Monday."

Generally speaking, the particle ni appears when one uses the prepositions in English, while it does not with words like "today; every day; usually" (kyoo, mai-nichi, taitee in Japanese, respectively). These words function as adverbs in such cases. Two of the exceptions are asa and yoru, which do not take ni although English counterparts take a preposition: "in the morning" and "in the evening; at night."

A place word + e corresponds to "to" in English as it indicates the "direction" toward which one moves. It is, therefore, used with motion verbs such as "to go," "to come," and "to return."

A place word + de "in; at" indicates a "place of action," in contrast to a place word + ni, which marks a "place of existence."

1. Watashi wa mai-asa shichi-ji ni okimasu.   "I get up at seven o'clock every morning."
2. Hachi-ji-goro(ni) toshokan e ikimasu.   "(I) go to the library around eight o'clock."
3. Taitee toshokan de hon o yomimasu.   "(I) usually read books in the library."
4. Toshokan ni hon ga takusan arimasu.   "There are many books in the library."

(B) The Word Order within a Sentence

Word order is relatively free in Japanese, as long as the verb comes at the end of a sentence. There is, however, "regular" order which carries no particular emphasis, as shown below. Any phrase (or phrases) except for the verb can be missing in a sentence. In the following, "ϕ" means "no particle." See Examples 4-7 above, also.

(SUBJECT wa/ga)　(TIME ni/ϕ)　(PLACE e)　MOTION VERB.
(SUBJECT wa/ga)　(TIME ni/ϕ)　(PLACE de)　(DIRECT OBJECT o)　VERB.

(C) Questions and Answers

To answer a "yes/no" question, repeat the verb in the affirmative or negative. "Ee, soo desu" and "Iie, chigaimasu" are inappropriate. In response to wh-questions (questions with "who," "what," "when," etc.), simply replace the question words with the information called for.

5. Q: たなかさんは まいにち としょかんへ いきますか。
"Do you (= Mr. Tanaka) go to the library every day?"
OR "Does Mr. Tanaka go to...?"

　A1: ええ、 いきます。
"Yes, I do." OR "Yes, he does."

　A2: いいえ、 いきません。
"No, I don't." OR "No, he doesn't."

6. Q: (まいにち) なんじに としょかんへ いきますか。
"What time do you go to the library (every day)?"

　A: よじに いきます。
"I go at four o'clock."

7. Q: よじに どこへ いきますか。
"Where do you go at four o'clock?"

　A: としょかんへ いきます。
"I go to the library."

8. Q: どこで しんぶんを よみますか。
"Where do you read the newspaper?"

　A: としょかんで よみます。
"I read it at the library."

9. Q: としょかんで なにを よみますか。
"What do you read at the library?"

　A: しんぶんを よみます。
"I read the newspaper."

10. Q: としょかんで なにを しますか。
"What do you do at the library?"

　A: しんぶんを よみます。
"I read the newspaper."

11. Q: だれが としょかんで しんぶんを よみますか。
"Who reads the newspaper at the library?"

　A: たなかさんが よみます。
"Mr. Tanaka does."

12. Q: (たなかさんは) なにごが わかりますか。　"What language do you understand?"
    A: (わたしは) ちゅうごくごが わかります。　"I understand Chinese."

    NOTE: The object of <u>wakaru</u> always takes <u>ga</u>, and not <u>o</u>.

(D) Verbal Nouns (VN) (compound verbs)

"Verbal nouns" are nouns which refer to actions rather than things. The great majority of these are loan words from Chinese (e.g., <u>benkyoo</u> "studying") while others are native Japanese words (e.g., <u>shigoto</u> "work") and words from other languages (e.g., <u>tenisu</u> "tennis").

When <u>shimasu</u> "to do" directly follows a verbal noun of Chinese origin, the entire phrase becomes a verb. On the other hand, when the particle <u>o</u> appears between a verbal noun and <u>shimasu</u>, it functions as a noun (a direct object). The meaning, however, is identical. Most verbal nouns of other origins as well as some Chinese ones require <u>o</u>, along with <u>shimasu</u>, in order to function as a verb.

13. a.　まいにち べんきょう します。　　"I study every day."

    b.　まいにち べんきょうを します。　Lit. "I do the study every day."

14. a.　にほんご を べんきょう します。　"I study Japanese."

    b.　にほんご の べんきょう を します。　Lit. "I do the study of Japanese."

III. Adverbs

"Adverbs" specify time, degree, frequency, quantity, manner in which an action is performed, and so forth. They appear <u>before</u> verbs, adjectives and other adverbs (as well as certain kinds of nouns) which they modify.

1. えんぴつが すこし あります。　　　　　"There are <u>a few</u> pencils."
   Lit. "Pencils exist scantily."

2. このがっこうに にほんじんが たくさん います。"There are <u>many</u> Japanese people in this school."

3. こどもは えいがを たくさん みます。　　"My child sees movies <u>a lot</u>."

4. a. もう くじです。　　　　　　　　　　"It's <u>already</u> nine o'clock."

   b. まだ くじです。　　　　　　　　　　"It's <u>still</u> nine o'clock."

5. a. まだ わかりません。　　　　　　　　"I don't know <u>yet</u>."
   OR "I <u>still</u> don't understand."

   b. もう わかりません。　　　　　　　　"I don't understand it <u>any more</u>."

IV. More Examples of 'wa' and 'mo' -- CONTRAST and SIMILARITY
cf. L.2, III. and L.3, I.

Semantic particles such as <u>wa</u> and <u>mo</u> can appear immediately <u>after</u> a grammatical particle (e.g., <u>ni</u>, <u>e</u>, <u>de</u>) to add the sense of "contrast" and "similarity," respectively. A semantic particle, however, replaces <u>ga</u> and <u>o</u>. (In most cases, two semantic particles or two grammatical particles cannot be combined in a sequence.)

It is very common for <u>wa</u> to appear in a negative sentence, though it is not restricted to it. The contrastive meaning is often expressed by stress and intonation in English. Be sure to put <u>wa</u> and <u>mo</u> immediately after the noun (plus another particle, if any) which is being compared.

1. a. わたしも あした ぎんこうへ いきます。 — "I, too, will go to the bank tomorrow."
   b. わたしは あしたも ぎんこうへ いきます。 — "I will go to the bank tomorrow, as well (as today, etc.)."
   c. わたしは あした ぎんこうへも いきます。 — "I will go to the bank as well (as to the post office, etc.) tomorrow."

2. がくせいが います。 — "The students are there."
   せんせいも います。 — "The teacher is there, too."
   OR せんせいは いません。 — "The teacher isn't there."

3. ほんを よみます。 — "I read books."
   ざっしも よみます。 — "I read magazines, too."
   OR ざっしは よみません。 — "I don't read magazines."

4. ここに いすが あります。 — "There is a chair here."
   あそこにも あります。 — "There is one over there, too."
   OR あそこには ありません。 — "There isn't any over there."

5. かいしゃで しごとを します。 — "I work in my office."
   うちでも しごとを します。 — "I work at home, too."
   OR うちでは しごとを しません。 — "I don't work at home."

6. どようびに べんきょう します。 — "I study on Saturdays."
   きんようびにも べんきょう します。 — "I study on Fridays, too."
   OR きんようびには べんきょう しません。 — "I don't study on Fridays."

7. あさ おちゃを のみます。 — "I drink tea in the morning."
   よるも のみます。 — "I drink it at night, too."
   OR よるは のみません。 — "I don't drink it at night."

第五課

Lesson 5 (だいごか): New Vocabulary

1.	X と Y	【P】	X and Y [JOINS NOUNS]	ほんと ざっしを よみます。
2.	X に NUMBER	【P】	...per/an X; for every X [STANDARD FOR FREQUENCY]	みっかに いちど いきます。 (one time)
3.	SENTENCE ね(え)。	【P】	..., isn't it! How ...! [SPEAKER'S AMAZEMENT]	はやいですねえ。
4.	SENTENCE よ。	【P】	..., you know. ..., I'm telling you! [EMPHASIS, FAMILIAR]	いい えいがが ありますよ。
5.	ふる	【u-V】	to fall [rain, snow]	あめが ふります。 (E.T.)が (Mo.)
6.	でかける	【ru-V】	to go out; to step out	こんばん でかけます。
7.	(Xを) やる	【u-V】	to do; play (sports, games) more vulgar / Don	しごとを やります。
Rev.	(Xを) する	【Ir.V】	to do; play (sports, games) [ADDITIONAL MEANING]	しごとを します。
*8.	(Xを) かう	【u-V】	to buy	かさを かいます。
9.	やきゅう	【VN】	baseball	やきゅうを します。
10.	すいえい	【VN】	swimming	すいえいを します。
11.	スポーツ (すぽーつ)	【VN】	sport(s)	スポーツを します。(すぽーつ)
12.	あめ	【N】	rain	あめですよ。
*13.	ゆき	【N】	snow	ゆきが ふります。
*14.	かみ	【N】	paper	しろい かみが あります。
15.	しょうせつ	【N】	novel	しょうせつを よみます。
16.	こうこう	【N】	high school	こうこうへ いきます。
17.	ばんぐみ	【N】	program (TV, radio)	いい ばんぐみを みます。
18.	こと	【N】	thing (which one does) [THINGS OF ABSTRACT NATURE: ACTIVITY, EVENT, ETC.]	いい ことを します。
*19.	テスト (てすと)	【N】	test	テストが あります。(てすと)
*20.	ステーキ (すてーき)	【N】	steak	ステーキを たべます。(すてーき)
*21.	サラダ (さらだ)	【N】	salad	サラダも たべます。(さらだ)
*22.	ビール (びーる)	【N】	beer	ビールを すこし のみます。(びーる)
*23.	ノート (のーと)	【N】	notebook	ノートを かいます。(のーと)
*24.	レコード (れこーど)	【N】	record	レコードが あります。(れこーど)
25.	よしだ	【N】	Yoshida [SURNAME]	
26.	さとう	【N】	Sato [SURNAME]	

27.	よしかわ	【N】	Yoshikawa [SURNAME]	
28.	なつめ そうせき	【N】	Soseki Natsume, a famous novelist	
29.	「こころ」	【N】	"The Heart of Things" (a novel by Soseki Natsume) <u>Kokoro</u> literally means "heart [NOT AS AN ORGAN]; mind"	
30.	きのう	【N,Ad】	yesterday	きのう いきました。
*31.	おととい	【N,Ad】	day before yesterday	おととい いきました。
32.	ゆうがた	【N,Ad】	early evening [4-6 p.m. or so]	ゆうがた かえります。
33.	(NOUN の) とき	【N,Ad】	at the time of/when; during...	こどもの とき みました。
*34.	どの ぐらい	【N,Ad】	to what extent; how many (much, long, etc.)	どのぐらい ねましたか。
35.	NUMBER ぐらい	【Suf】	about... [APPROXIMATE AMOUNT AND TIME SPAN]	にじかんぐらい ねました。
36.	NOUN じゅう	【Suf】	throughout..; all through (time period)	いちにちじゅう ねました。
37.	こんな + NOUN	【Pren】	this kind/type of...	こんな ほんを よみます。
38.	そんな + NOUN	【Pren】	that kind/type of... [ONLY ONE PARTY KNOWS IT]	そんな ほんを よみます。
39.	あんな + NOUN	【Pren】	that kind/type of... [BOTH THE SPEAKER AND THE LISTENER KNOW IT]	あんな ほんを よみます。
40.	どんな + NOUN	【Pren】	what kind/type of...	どんな ほんを よみますか。
41.	いろいろ(な)	【na-A】	various; all kinds of	いろいろな ほんを よみます。
42.	たかい	【i-A】	high; expensive	この くつは たかいですねえ。
43.	よく + VERB	【Ad】	often; a lot; well	よく ゆきが ふります。
44.	あまり + VERB あまり + ADJ/ADV	【Ad】	(not) often; (not) much; (not) very...	あまり ゆきが ふりません。
45.	でも	【Conj】	but; however	A: いい とけいですね。 B: ええ、でも、すこし たかいです。

Numbers and Counters:

(A) ～さつ: bound objects -- books, dictionaries, notebooks, photo albums

1: いっさつ　　2: にさつ　　3: さんさつ　　4: よんさつ　　5: ごさつ
6: ろくさつ　　7: ななさつ　8: はっさつ　　9: きゅうさつ　　10: じっさつ
11: じゅういっさつ ...　　20: にじっさつ　　　　　　なんさつ "how many"

(B) ～まい: thin, flat objects -- records, paper, slices, sheets, plates

1: いちまい　　2: にまい　　3: さんまい　　4: よ(ん)まい　　5: ごまい
6: ろくまい　　7: ななまい　8: はちまい　　9: きゅうまい　　10: じゅうまい
11: じゅういちまい ...　　20: にじゅうまい　　　　　なんまい "how many"

本 (C) ～ほん/ぼん/ぽん: long, cylindrical objects -- pens, pencils, bottles, stalks, umbrellas, trees. See ...<u>hyaku</u> for h/b/p alternation (L.2).

    1: いっ<u>ぽ</u>ん   2: に<u>ほ</u>ん   3: さん<u>ぼ</u>ん   4: よん<u>ほ</u>ん   5: ご<u>ほ</u>ん
    6: ろっ<u>ぽ</u>ん   7: なな<u>ほ</u>ん   8: はっ<u>ぽ</u>ん   9: きゅう<u>ほ</u>ん   10: じっ<u>ぽ</u>ん
    11: じゅういっ<u>ぽ</u>ん ...   20: にじっ<u>ぽ</u>ん   なん<u>ぼ</u>ん "how many"

時間 (D) ～じかん: ...hours (～じ "...o'clock" + かん SUFFIX FOR DURATION OF TIME)

    1: いちじかん   2: にじかん   3: さんじかん   4: <u>よ</u>じかん   5: ごじかん...
    9: <u>く</u>じかん...   11: じゅういちじかん ...   なんじかん "how many hours"

日(間) (E) ～か/にち: ...days; days of the month

Only <u>ichi-nichi</u> "one day" and <u>tsuitachi</u> "the first day of the month" are different. -<u>Kan</u> may be added after -<u>ka</u>/-<u>nichi</u> to explicitly express duration of time, e.g., <u>hutsu-ka</u>(-<u>kan</u>) "two days."

    1: ついたち/いちにち   11: じゅういちにち   21: にじゅういちにち
    2: ふつか   12: じゅうににち   22: にじゅうににち
    3: みっか   13: じゅうさんにち   23: にじゅうさんにち
    4: よっか   14: じゅう<u>よっか</u>   24: にじゅう<u>よっか</u>
    5: いつか   15: じゅうごにち   25: にじゅうごにち
    6: むいか   16: じゅうろくにち   26: にじゅうろくにち
    7: なのか   17: じゅう<u>しち</u>にち   ....
    8: ようか   18: じゅうはちにち
    9: ここのか   19: じゅう<u>く</u>にち   なんにち "how many days;
    10: とおか   20: はつか   what's the date?"

(F) ～しゅうかん: ...weeks. See (A) above for the occurrence of double 's' sounds.

    1: いっしゅうかん   2: にしゅうかん   3: さんしゅうかん...   なんしゅうかん
    "how many weeks"

(G) ～ねん: ...years; the year... (-<u>Kan</u> can be added for duration of time.)

    1: いちねん   2: にねん   3: さんねん   4: <u>よ</u>ねん...   なんねん "what year;
the year 1987: せんきゅうひゃくはちじゅうななねん   how many years"

(H) ～ど: ...times [FREQUENCY] e.g. もう いち<u>ど</u> "one more time; once again"

    1: いちど   2: にど   3: さんど   4: よ(ん)ど...   なんど "how many times"

(I) ～か: ...lessons; lesson...

    1: いっか   2: にか   3: さんか...   なんか "how many lessons; what lesson"

Translation of the Examples:

1. I read books and magazines.
2. I go (there) once every three days.
3. Wow, that's early, isn't it.
4. There is a good movie, you know. [IMPLIES: I bet you didn't know that.]
5. It rains.
6. I'll go out tonight.
7. I work. [Lit. I do the work.]
Rev. I work. [Lit. I do the work.]
8. I'll buy an umbrella.
9. I play baseball.
10. I swim.
11. I do (OR play) sports.
12. It's rain!
13. It snows.
14. There is some white paper.
15. I read novels.
16. I will go to high school.
17. I watch good programs.
18. He/She does good things.
19. There is a test.
20. I eat steak.
21. I eat salad, too.
22. I drink a little beer.
23. I buy notebooks.
24. There is a record.
30. I went (there) yesterday.
31. I went (there) the day before yesterday.
32. I will return in the early evening.
33. I saw it when I was a child.
34. How long did you sleep?
35. I slept for about two hours.
36. I slept all day.
37. I read this kind of book.
38. I read that kind of book. [AS I (OR YOU) JUST REFERRED TO]
39. I read that kind of book. [WITH WHICH YOU ARE FAMILIAR]
40. What kind of books do you read?
41. I read various books.
42. These shoes are expensive!
43. It snows often (OR a lot).
44. It doesn't snow often (OR much).
45. A: Nice watch, isn't it.
    B: Yes, but it's a little expensive.

Lesson 5: Grammar

I. The Past Tense Form of Verbs (in polite style)

The past tense is indicated by -ta, which appears at the end of a verb.

All verbs: Affimative: ...masu → ...mashita "did..."
            Negative: ...masen → ...masen-deshita "did not do..."

1. Q: きのう がっこうへ いきましたか。 "Did you go to school yesterday?"
   A1: ええ、いきました。 "Yes, I did."
   A2: いいえ、いきませんでした。 "No, I didn't."

2. Q: きのうは なにを しましたか。 "What did you do yesterday?"
   A: りょうで テレビを みました。 "I watched TV in the dormitory."

As shown in Example 2 above, a time word such as kinoo "yesterday" can be the topic of a sentence and followed by wa -- "as for yesterday, ..." The subject, in this case ...san wa, "you," can also be added initially.

II. Yoku (...AFF.) vs. Amari (...NEG.)   "(do) often/a lot" vs. "(do not do) often/much"

Yoku and amari are adverbs indicating degrees of frequency. Remember that amari can only be used in a negative sentence.

1. a. よく きっさてんへ いきます。 "I go to coffee shops often."
   b. あまり きっさてんへ いきません。 "I don't go to coffee shops (that) often."

2. Q: こどもの とき、よく スポーツを しましたか。 "When you were a child, did you do sports a lot?"
   [cf. いろいろな スポーツ "many sports"]
   A1: ええ、(よく) しました。 "Yes, I did (a lot)."
   A2: いいえ、あまり しませんでした。 "No, I didn't do much."

3. きのうは あめが よく ふりましたねえ。 "It rained a lot yesterday, didn't it."
   [IN THE SENSE THAT "it kept on raining"]

III. Numbers and Counters   cf. pp.29-30

(A) Time Expressions

Specific "point in time" takes the particle ni, but "duration of time" does not. Use -goro for an approximate point in time and -gurai "about..." for an approximate time duration and amount. Ni is optional with -goro.

-Kan denotes duration of time. For example, ichi-ji means "one o'clock" whereas ichi-ji-kan is "one hour." It is obligatory with "hours" and "weeks," but optional with "days" and "years."

1. a. くじに ねます。   "I go to bed at nine." [POINT IN TIME]
   b. くじかん ねます。   "I sleep for nine hours." [DURATION]
2. a. みっかに にほんへ いきます。   "I'll go to Japan on the third."
   b. にほんに みっか(かん) います。   "I'll stay in Japan for three days."
3. a. せんきゅうひゃくはちじゅうねんごろ(に) ここへ きました。   "I came here around (the year) 1980."
   b. ここに いちねん(かん)ぐらい いました。   "I was here for about a year."

In addition to "place of existence" and specific "point in time," the particle ni indicates "standard of frequency" -- "per...; a...; for every..."

4. いちにちに さんど ごはんを たべます。   "I eat meals three times a day."
5. いっしゅうかんに にど でかけます。   "I go out twice a week."
6. さんかに いちど テストが あります。   "There is a test (once) for every three lessons."

(B) Amount Expressions

When counting things, you need to attach a special "counter" to the number depending on the shape or nature of the object. The counters are similar to English expressions such as one cup of coffee, two sheets of paper, three bottles of beer.

The combination of a number + a counter (an amount word) functions as an adverb. Grammatical particles such as ga and o are attached to the noun, and not to the amount word, which usually appears between the noun and the verb: NOUN-PARTICLE + AMOUNT + VERB.

7. ほんが にさつ あります。   "There are two books."
8. Q: ほんを なんさつ よみましたか。   "How many books did you read?"
   A: にさつ よみました。   "I read two."
9. Q: えんぴつを なんぼんぐらい かいますか。(OR どのぐらい)   "About how many pencils are you going to buy?"
   A: ごほんぐらい かいます。   "I'm going to buy about five."
10. Q: レコードは たくさん ありますか。   "Do you have many records?"
    A: ええ、ひゃくまいぐらい あります。   "Yes, I have about a hundred."

IV. QW + 'ka' vs. QW + 'mo'   "some...; any..." vs. "(not) any..."

A question word + <u>ka</u> is a noun meaning, "some..." or "any..." (in a question). A question word + <u>mo</u> is used only in a negative sentence to indicate total negation, "(not) any..." Questions with these words are answered with "yes" or "no."

The particles <u>ga</u> and <u>o</u> are usually deleted with QW + <u>ka</u>, and always deleted with QW + <u>mo</u>. Other grammatical particles such as <u>e</u>, <u>ni</u> and <u>de</u>, however, remain.

なに "what"	なにか "something"	なにも (...Neg.) "(not) anything"
だれ "who"	だれか "someone"	だれも (...Neg.) "(not) anyone"
どこ "where"	どこかへ "to some place"	どこへも (...Neg.) "(not) to any place"
	どこかに "in some place"	どこにも (...Neg.) "(not) in any place"
	どこかで "at some place"	

1. Q: <u>なにか</u>(<u>が</u>) ありますか。   "Is there anything/something?"
   A1: ええ、かさ<u>が</u> あります。   "Yes, there is an umbrella."
   A2: いいえ、<u>なにも</u> ありません。   "No, there isn't anything."
   cf. <u>なにが</u> ありますか。   "What is there?"

2. Q: <u>だれか</u>(<u>が</u>) いますか。   "Is there anyone/someone?"
   A1: ええ、やましたさん<u>が</u> います。   "Yes, Mr. Yamashita is there."
   A2: いいえ、<u>だれも</u> いません。   "No, there isn't anyone."
   cf. <u>だれが</u> いますか   "Who is there?"

3. Q: <u>なにか</u>(<u>を</u>) のみましたか。   "Did you drink anything/something?"
   A1: ええ、みず<u>を</u> のみました。   "Yes, I drank some water."
   A2: いいえ、<u>なにも</u> のみませんでした。   "No, I didn't drink anything."
   cf. <u>なにを</u> のみましたか。   "What did you drink?"

4. Q: <u>どこかへ</u> いきましたか。   "Did you go anywhere/somewhere?"
   A1: ええ、きょうかい<u>へ</u> いきました。   "Yes, I went to church."
   A2: いいえ、<u>どこへも</u> いきませんでした。   "No, I didn't go anywhere."
   cf. <u>どこへ</u> いきましたか。   "Where did you go?"

5. Q: ノートは どこかに ありましたか。　　"Did you find your notebook anywhere?"
　　　　　　　　　　　　　　　　　　　　　　Lit. "Was your notebook anywhere?"

　　A1: ええ、いすの したに ありました。　　"Yes, it was under the chair."

　　A2: いいえ、どこにも ありませんでした。　"No, I didn't find it anywhere."
　　　　　　　　　　　　　　　　　　　　　　Lit. "No, it wasn't anywhere."

　　cf. ノートは どこに ありましたか。　　　"Where was your notebook?"

6. Q: どこかで ごはんを たべましたか。　　　"Did you eat dinner anywhere?"

　　A: ええ、しょくどうで たべました。　　　"Yes, I ate in the dining room."

　　(YOU CANNOT SAY: どこでも たべませんでした。)

　　cf. どこで ごはんを たべましたか。　　　"Where did you eat dinner?"

V. Ko-So-A-Do Words -- Out of Sight

Ko-so-a-do words are used to refer to abstract notions and objects that are out of sight, in addition to referring to objects in sight.

Sore refers to subject matter about which only one party knows. Are refers to subject matter with which both the speaker and the listener are familiar. Other so- and a- words follow the same principle both in speech and in writing.

1. A: きのう「こころ」を よみました。　　　"I read Kokoro yesterday."

　　B1: それ は いい しょうせつですか。　　"Is that a good novel?"
　　　　　　　　　　　　　　　　　　　　　　['B' HAS NOT HEARD ABOUT THE NOVEL.]

　　B2: あれ は いい しょうせつですね。　　"That is a good novel, isn't it?"
　　　　　　　　　　　　　　　　　　　　　　['B' HAS HEARD ABOUT THE NOVEL.]

2. A: おととい さとうさんが きました。　　　"Ms. Sato came the day before yesterday."

　　B1: そのひとは どんな ひとですか。　　　"What is that person like?"
　　　　　　　　　　　　　　　　　　　　　　['B' DOES NOT KNOW MS. SATO.]

　　B2: あのひとは いい ひとですね。　　　　"She (Lit. that person) is a nice person,
　　　　　　　　　　　　　　　　　　　　　　isn't she." ['B' KNOWS MS. SATO.]

3. Example from a written passage:

　　きのう きっさてんへ いきました。　　　　"I went to a coffee shop yesterday.
　　そこで おちゃを のみました。　　　　　　There I had some tea."

In writing, asoko, are and ano- usually cannot be used because the information is not commonly shared between the writer and the reader.

Lesson 6 (だいろっか): New Vocabulary

1.	CLAUSE が、CLAUSE.	【P】	..., but...	でかけましたが、すぐ かえりました。
2.	NOUN に (あう)	【P】	[TARGET/INDIRECT OBJECT]	だれに あいますか。
3.	(Xに) あう	【u-V】	to see (a person); meet	スミスさんに あいます。
4.	たりる	【ru-V】	to be enough; be sufficient	かみが たりません。
5.	はなす	【u-V】	to talk; speak; chat	りょうで はなしました。
6.	はなし	【VN】	story; talk; chat	りょうで はなしを しました。
7.	パーティー	【VN】	party	パーティーが あります。
*8.	アパート	【N】	apartment; apt. building	いい アパートですね。
9.	かいじょう	【N】	place of meeting/exhibit	かいじょうは どこですか。
10.	ともだち	【N】	friend	にほんに ともだちが います。
11.	にく	【N】	meat	にくは たかいです。
*12.	とりにく	【N】	chiken (meat); poultry	とりにくを たべます。
*13.	やさい	【N】	vegetable	やさいも たべます。
14.	さかな	【N】	fish	さかなは あまり たべません。
*15.	たまご	【N】	egg	たまごが すこし あります。
16.	みせ	【N】	store; shop	あの みせで かいました。
17.	びょうき	【N】	ill(ness); sick; disease [cf. byoo-in]	たなかさんは びょうきです。
18.	じかん	【N】	time	じかんが ありません。
19.	ところ	【N】	place	どんな ところですか。
20.	もの	【N】	thing [TANGIBLE]; object	いろいろな ものを かいます。
21.	やまもと	【N】	Yamamoto [SURNAME]	
22.	こばやし	【N】	Kobayashi [SURNAME]	
23.	まつもと	【N】	Matsumoto [SURNAME]	
24.	もり	【N】	Mori [SURNAME]	
25.	しんじゅく	【N】	Shinjuku [PLACE NAME, A SECTION IN TOKYO]	
26.	このごろ	【N,Ad】	these days; recently	このごろ あめが よく ふります。
27.	はやく + VERB	【Ad】	(do...) early; fast [ADVERBIAL FORM OF hayai]	まいあさ はやく おきます。
28.	おそく + VERB	【Ad】	(do...) late [ADVERBIAL FORM OF osoi]	まいばん おそく ねます。
29.	こう	【Ad】	this way; in this manner	① こうします。 ② こうです。
30.	そう	【Ad】	that way; in that manner [AS THE SPEAKER OR THE LISTENER HAS JUST INDICATED]	① そうします。 ② そうです。

31. ああ	【Ad】	that way; in that manner	① ああ します。 ② ああです。	
		[WITH WHICH THE SPEAKER <u>AND</u> THE LISTENER ARE FAMILIAR]		
32. どう	【Ad】	how (about); in what manner [QW]	① どう しますか。	
			② どうですか。	
33. いかが	【Ad】	how (about); in what manner [QW]	あしたは いかがですか。	
		[MORE POLITE THAN <u>doo</u>]		
34. どうして	【Ad】	why; how come [QW]	どうしてですか。	
35. おおきい	【i-A】	large; big	おおきい かばんです。	
*36. ちいさい	【i-A】	small [Opp. <u>ookii</u>]	ちいさい かばんです。	
37. やすい	【i-A】	inexpensive; cheap [Opp. <u>takai</u>]	やすい とけいです。	
38. あたらしい	【i-A】	new; fresh	あたらしい たてものです。	
*39. ふるい	【i-A】	old [NOT SOMEONE'S AGE] [Opp. <u>atarashii</u>]	ふるい たてものです。	
*40. おいしい	【i-A】	delicious; tastes good	おいしい にくです。	
41. ひろい	【i-A】	spacious; wide	ひろい アパートです。	
42. いそがしい	【i-A】	busy (many things to do)	いそがしい ひとです。	
43. ひま(な)	【na-A】	free; have free time [Opp. <u>isogashii</u>]	ひまな ひとです。	
44. しずか(な)	【na-A】	quiet	しずかな ところです。	
45. にぎやか(な)	【na-A】	lively; bustling; busy (place) [Opp. <u>shizuka</u>]	にぎやかな ところです。	
46. きれい(な)	【na-A】	pretty; clean	きれいな ひとです。	
47. りっぱ(な)	【na-A】	stately; impressive	りっぱな うちです。	
48. げんき(な)	【na-A】	healthy; well; full of energy; high-sprited	げんきな こどもです。	
49. たいへん(な)	【na-A】	tough; rough; hectic	たいへんな しごとです。	
50. ざんねん(な)	【na-A】	regrettable; sorry; too bad	ざんねんな ことです。	
51. せん 〜	【Pref】	last...	せんしゅう	
52. こん 〜	【Pref】	this... [cf. <u>kon-nichi wa</u>.]	こんしゅう	
53. らい 〜	【Pref】	next...	らいしゅう、らいねん	
54. NOUN や	【Suf】	...store; ...shop	ほんや、くつや、にくや	
55. じゃ	【Conj】	well then; in that case	A: これは たかいですよ。	
			B: じゃ、かいません。	

Numbers and Counters:

(A) 〜ふん/ぷん：　...minutes

1: いっぷん	2: にふん	3: さんぷん	4: よんぷん	5: ごふん
6: ろっぷん	7: ななふん	8: はっぷん	9: きゅうふん	10: じっぷん

15: じゅうごふん ... 20: にじっぷん ... 25: にじゅうごふん ... なんぷん "how many minutes"

(B) ～がつ: names of the months (not for counting months)

Jan.: いちがつ　Feb.: にがつ　Mar.: さんがつ　Apr.: しがつ　May: ごがつ
Jun.: ろくがつ　Jul.: しちがつ　Aug.: はちがつ　Sep.: くがつ　Oct.: じゅうがつ
Nov.: じゅういちがつ　Dec.: じゅうにがつ　　　　　　なんがつ "what month"

Translation of the Examples:

1. I went out, but returned immediately.
2. Whom will you see?
3. I will see Mr./Ms. Smith.
4. There isn't enough paper.
5. We talked in the dormitory.
6. We talked in the dormitory.
7. There is a party.
8. Nice apartment, isn't it.
9. Where is the place of the meeting?
10. I have a friend in Japan.
11. Meat is expensive.
12. I eat chicken.
13. I eat vegetables, too.
14. I don't eat fish much.
15. There are some eggs.
16. I bought it at that store.
17. Mr./Ms. Tanaka is ill.
18. There isn't time.
19. What kind of place is it?
20. I buy various things.
26. It rains a lot these days.
27. I get up early every morning.
28. I go to bed late every night.
29. ① I do it this way.
    ② It's like this.
30. ① I do it that way.
    ② It's like that. (OR That's right.)
31. ① I do it that way.
    ② It's like that.
32. ① How do you do it?
    ② How is it?
33. How is (OR How about) tomorrow?
34. Why? (OR Why not?)
35. It's a large bag.
36. It's a small bag.
37. It's an inexpensive watch.
38. It's a new building.
39. It's an old building.
40. It's delicious meat.
41. It's a spacious apartment.
42. He/She is a busy person.
43. He/She has nothing to do.
44. It's a quiet place.
45. It's a bustling place.
46. She is a pretty woman (person).
47. It's a stately house.
48. He/She is a healthy child.
49. It's a tough job.
50. It's a regrettable thing.
51. last week
52. this week
53. next week, next year
54. book store, shoe store, meat shop
55. A: This is expensive, you know.
    B: Then I won't buy it.

Lesson 6: Grammar

I. Conjugation of i-Type Adjectives and the Copula

I-type adjectives in Japanese are like verbs in that they are conjugated. Desu attached to i-adjectives merely indicates politeness, and i- itself expresses the present tense. Desu with na-adjectives and nouns, on the other hand, is called the "copula" and are conjugated like the be-verb "is; am; are." Na-type adjectives themselves, therefore, are not conjugated and are similar to nouns in all respects except in their noun-modifying form.

(A) The Stem of an Adjective

The "stem" refers to the part of an adjective that is constant, i.e., an i-adjective minus i, and a na-adjective minus na. For example, the stem of takai "expensive" is taka and the stem of kiree na "pretty; clean" is kiree.

(B) The Noun-Modifying Form (the form used to modify a noun)

i-ADJ:	これは	たか	い	ほんです。	"This is an expensive book."
na-ADJ:	これは	きれい	な	ほんです。	"This is a pretty book."
NOUN :	これは	こども	の	ほんです。	"This is a children's book."

(C) The Sentence-Final Form (the form used at the end of a sentence)

The past negative form is obtained by changing the PRESENT negative form into the past, not from past affirmative to the negative.

i-ADJ: Pres. Aff.: これは たかいです。   "This is expensive."
       Pres. Neg.: これは たかく ありません。   "This is not expensive."
       Past Aff.: これは たかかったです。   "This was expensive."
       Past Neg.: これは たかく ありませんでした。 "This was not expensive."

EXCEPTION: いい "good"   (The stem is yo, not i.)

   Pres. Aff.: これは いいです。   "This is good."
   Pres. Neg.: これは よく ありません。   "This is not good."
   Past Aff.: これは よかったです。   "This was good."
   Past Neg.: これは よく ありませんでした。   "This was not good."

na-ADJ: Pres. Aff.: アパートは きれいです。   "The apartment is clean."
        Pres. Neg.: アパートは きれいじゃ ありません。   "The apt. is not clean."
        Past Aff.: アパートは きれいでした。   "The apartment was clean."
        Past Neg.: アパートは きれいじゃ ありませんでした。 "The apartment was not clean."

NOUN:
Pres. Aff.: たなかさんは がくせい<u>です</u>。 "Mr. Tanaka <u>is</u> a student."
Pres. Neg.: たなかさんは がくせい<u>じゃ ありません</u>。 "Mr. Tanaka <u>is</u> <u>not</u> a student."
Past Aff.: たなかさんは がくせい<u>でした</u>。 "Mr. Tanaka <u>was</u> a student."
Past Neg.: たなかさんは がくせい<u>じゃ ありませんでした</u>。 "Mr. Tanaka <u>was</u> <u>not</u> a student."

(D) The -Te Form: 'kute' and 'de'   "..., and..."

The <u>-te</u> form of an adjective and the copula is used to connect it with another adjective (of either type) or with a verb. The form does not carry tenses; its tense is usually considered the same as the one indicated at the end of a sentence. The <u>-te</u> form of an i-adjective is stem + <u>kute</u>, while that of the copula (<u>desu</u>) is <u>de</u>, i.e., <u>na</u>-adjective stem + <u>de</u> and noun + <u>de</u>. Remember that the particle <u>to</u> can only connect nouns to form a noun phrase.

i-ADJ:
1. a. たか<u>くて</u> おおきい うち<u>です</u>。 "It <u>is</u> an expensive <u>and</u> big house."
   b. たか<u>くて</u> おおきい うち<u>でした</u>。 "It <u>was</u> an expensive <u>and</u> big house."
   c. うちは たか<u>くて</u> おおき<u>いです</u>。 "The house <u>is</u> expensive <u>and</u> big."
   d. うちは たか<u>くて</u> おおき<u>かったです</u>。 "The house <u>was</u> expensive <u>and</u> big."

na-ADJ:
2. a. きれい<u>で</u> しずかな うち<u>です</u>。 "It <u>is</u> a pretty <u>and</u> quiet house."
   b. きれい<u>で</u> しずかな うち<u>でした</u>。 "It <u>was</u> a pretty <u>and</u> quiet house."
   c. うちは きれい<u>で</u> しずか<u>です</u>。 "The house <u>is</u> pretty <u>and</u> quiet."
   d. うちは きれい<u>で</u> しずか<u>でした</u>。 "The house <u>was</u> pretty <u>and</u> quiet."

NOUN:
3. a. たなかさんは がくせい<u>で</u>、おくさんは せんせい<u>です</u>。 "Mr. Tanaka <u>is</u> a student, <u>and</u> his wife <u>is</u> a teacher."
   b. これは ひゃくえん<u>で</u>、あれは せんえん<u>でした</u>。 "This <u>was</u> 100 yen, <u>and</u> that <u>was</u> 1,000 yen."
   c. よしださんは びょうき<u>で</u>、パーティへ <u>きませんでした</u>。 "Mr. Yoshida <u>was</u> sick, <u>and did</u> <u>not</u> come to the party."

(E) Questions and Answers

To answer a "yes/no" question, repeat the adjective in the affirmative or negative. "<u>Ee, soo desu</u>" and "<u>Iie, chigaimasu</u>" should be used only when the question ends with "<u>NOUN desu ka</u>." Furthermore, you cannot simply replace the question word <u>doo</u> "how" with an adjective in your answers; consider what form is appropriate in each situation.

1. Q: ステーキは おいしいですか。 "Is the steak good?"
   A1: ええ、おいしいです。 "Yes, it is."
   A2: いいえ、おいしく ありません。 "No, it isn't."

2. Q: やましたさんは げんきでしたか。 "Was Mr. Yamashita well?"
   A1: ええ、げんきでした。 "Yes, he was."
   A2: いいえ、あまり げんきじゃ ありませんでした。 "No, he wasn't very well."

3. Q: パーティーは どうでしたか。 "How was the party?"
   A: にぎやかで、よかったですよ。 "It was lively and nice."

4. Q: あたらしい しごとは どうですか。 "How is your new job?"
   A: いそがしくて、たいへんです。 "It keeps me busy and it's tough."

II. CLAUSE (X) ga, CLAUSE (Y)   "X, but Y." "Y although X." "X while Y."

Ga is a conjunctive particle attached to the first clause and the whole constitutes one sentence. In contrast, demo "however" can only be used at the beginning of a sentence. Note that commas appear after ga, not before it.

1. よしかわさんは しごとを しましたが、なかむらさんは しませんでした。 "Mr. Yoshikawa worked, but Mr. Nakamura didn't."

cf. よしださんは しごとを しました。でも、なかむらさんは しませんでした。 "Mr. Yoshida worked. However, Mr. Nakamura didn't."

2. きのうは あめが ふりましたが、きょうは いい てんきです。 "It rained yesterday, but it's sunny today."

3. りょうは ふるいですが、いいです。 "The dormitory is old, but it's nice."

cf. りょうは ふるくて、いいです。 "The dormitory is old, and it's nice."

In speech, though not in writing, the order of the two clauses is often reversed. Instead of the regular order of "X ga, Y," you can say, "Y. X ga."

4. a. きょうは いきませんが、あしたは いきます。 "I won't go today, but I will go tomorrow."
   b. あしたは いきます。きょうは いきませんが。 "I will go tomorrow. I'm not going today, though."

III. Negative Questions

Hai and ee mean "what you just said is right" and iie means "what you just said is wrong," regardless of whether the question is in the affirmative or negative (which anticipates a negative answer). Therefore, with <u>hai</u> or <u>ee</u> you say basically the same thing as in the question, whereas with <u>iie</u> you say something different.

1. Q: べんきょうを し<u>ません</u>でしたか。 "Did you <u>not</u> (OR Did<u>n't</u> you) study?"
   A1: <u>はい</u>、しませんでした。 "<u>No</u> (Lit. Right), I didn't."
   A2: <u>いいえ</u>、しました。 "<u>Yes</u>, I did study."

2. Q: あのひとは にほんじん<u>じゃ ありません</u>ね。 "That man isn't Japanese, is he?"
   A1: <u>ええ</u>、にほんじんじゃ ありません。 "<u>Right</u>. He isn't."
   A2: <u>いいえ</u>、にほんじんですよ。 "<u>No</u>, he is Japanese!"

IV. <u>Choice Questions</u>   "Is it X, or Y?" "Do you do X, or Y?" etc.

When you ask a choice question in Japanese, simply repeat two (or more) questions. The intonation rises at the end of both (or all) questions.

1. Q: やすみは どようび<u>ですか</u>、にちようび<u>ですか</u>。 "Is your holiday on Saturday, <u>or</u> Sunday?"
   A: にちようびです。 "It's on Sunday."

2. Q: こんばんは しごとの あと すぐ うちへ かえります<u>か</u>、どこかへ でかけますか。 "Are you going home right after work tonight, <u>or</u> are you going out somewhere?"
   A: まだ わかりません。 "I don't know yet."

V. <u>Numbers and Counters</u>   cf. pp.37-38

1. Q: いま <u>なんぷん</u>ですか。 "How many minutes (past the hour) is it now?"
   A: <u>よんぷん</u>です。 "It's four minutes (past the hour)."

2. a. いま にじ <u>じゅうごふん</u>(すぎ)です。 "It's quarter past two now."
   b. いま にじ <u>じゅうごふんまえ</u>です。 "It's quarter to two now."

3. a. えいがは <u>にじっぷんごろ</u>(に) おわります。 "The movie will end at around 20 minutes (past the hour)."
   b. うちで <u>にじっぷんぐらい</u> ねます。 "I'll sleep for about 20 minutes at home."

4. Q: きょうは (<u>なんがつ</u>) <u>なんにち</u>ですか。 "What's the date today?"
   A: <u>しがつ ここのか</u>です。 "It's April 9th."

5. <u>しちがつに</u> にほんへ いきます。 "I'm going to Japan in July."

VI. Others

(A) X に あいます   "to see X; meet (with) X; run into X"

Au/aimasu is an intransitive verb and, therefore, it cannot take the particle o, but must take ni which indicates the "target" (and "indirect object"). This particle can also replace e for "direction"; ni can be used wherever e is used, but not vice versa.

1. Q: あした こばやしさんに あいますか。   "Will you see Mr. Kobayashi tomorrow?"
   A: ええ、あいます。   "Yes, I will."

2. Q: ぎんこうで だれかに あいましたか。   "Did you run into anyone at the bank?"
   A: いいえ、だれにも あいませんでした。   "No, I didn't run into anyone."

3. いっしゅうかんに いちど きょうかいに いきます。   (OR へ)   "I go to church once a week."

(B) はなします vs. はなしを します   "to talk; speak; chat" cf. L.4, II-D.

To express the meaning, "speak a language," you must say ...o hanasu/hanashimasu and not hanashi o suru/shimasu. The two expressions are otherwise interchangeable although there are slight differences as shown below.

1. うちで ときどき かんこくごを はなします。   "I sometimes speak Korean at home."
2. いちにちじゅう はなしを しました (OR はなしました)。 "We talked all day."
3. Q: なんの (OR どんな) はなしを しましたか。 "What did you talk about?"
   OR どんな ことを はなしましたか。

   A1: やきゅうの はなしを しました。   "We talked about baseball."
   A2: いろいろな はなしを しました。   "We talked about various things."
   OR やきゅうの ことを はなしました。   [SAME AS ABOVE]
       いろいろな ことを はなしました。

(C) The Use of the Question Mark (?)

In Japanese the question mark is used only when transcribing incomplete questions. The question mark signals that the intonation must rise at the end of the phrase when one reads it.

1. すずき: このごろは どうですか。 いそがしいですか。   "How are things these days? Are you busy?"
   たなか: ええ、いそがしいです。   "Yes, I am.
       すずきさんは？ [どうですか IS OMITTED]   And (how about) you?"

- 43 -

Lesson 7 (だいななか): New Vocabulary

1.	(Xを) きく	【u-V】	to listen to; hear X	レコードを ききます。
	(Xに) きく		to ask X	せんせいに ききます。
2.	(Xを) つかう	【u-V】	to use X	ペンを つかいます。
3.	(Xを) まつ	【u-V】	to wait for X	ともだちを まちます。
4.	(Xを) つつむ	【u-V】	to wrap X	はこを つつみます。
5.	(Xを) よぶ	【u-V】	to call/summon; invite X	すずきさんを よびます。
6.	しぬ	【u-V】	to die	ねこが しにました。
7.	いそぐ	【u-V】	to hurry; be in a hurry	いそぎますか。
8.	たつ	【u-V】	to stand up	こどもが たちました。
9.	やくに たつ	【Phr】	to be helpful; be useful	じしょは やくに たちます。
*10.	がんばる	【u-V】	to try one's best; persevere	がんばります。
11.	たすかる	【u-V】	to be saved; be helped out	たすかりました。
12.	(Xに) あがる	【u-V】	to go up to/on X; enter a (Japanese-style) house	いすの うえに あがります。
13.	(Xに) はいる	【u-V】	to enter; go into X	きょうしつに はいります。
	(おちゃが) はいる		(tea, coffee) is made/poured	おちゃが はいりましたよ。
14.	(Xに Yを) いれる	【ru-V】	to put/pour Y into X	かばんに ほんを いれます。
	(おちゃを) いれる		to make (tea, coffee)	おちゃを いれます。
15.	(Xに Yを) つける	【ru-V】	to attach; put Y on X	はこに リボンを つけます。
	(テレビを) つける		to turn on TV (radio, etc.)	テレビを つけました。
16.	(Xに Yを) あげる	【ru-V】	to give Y to X [TO OTHERS WHO ARE ONE'S EQUAL]	ともだちに ほんを あげます。
17.	(Xに Yを) さしあげる	【ru-V】	(I humbly) give Y to X [TO MY SUPERIOR]	せんせいに さしあげます。
*18.	(Xに) こたえる	【ru-V】	to answer X	しつもんに こたえます。
Rev.	しつれい する	【suru】	to excuse oneself; (I humbly) leave	すぐ しつれい しました。
19.	りんご	【N】	apple	まいにち りんごを たべます。
20.	みかん	【N】	mandarin orange; tangerine	この みかんは おいしいです。
21.	メロン	【N】	melon	メロンは たかいです。
22.	くだもの	【N】	fruit	くだものやが あります。
23.	リボン	【N】	ribbon	きれいな リボンですね。

24.	ラジオ	【N】	radio		あさは ラジオを ききます。
*25.	テープ	【N】	tape		にほんごの テープを ききます。
*26.	ラボ	【N】	language laboratory		ラボで テープを ききました。
27.	きっぷ	【N】	ticket		ちかてつの きっぷを かいました。
28.	さんこうしょ	【N】	reference book		さんこうしょを よみました。
29.	おたく	【N】	(other's) house; residence [POLITE]		せんせいの おたくへ いきました。
30.	こうえん	【N】	park		こうえんで やきゅうを やります。

			LITERALLY --	POLITE FOR --	
31.	こちら	【N】	this way/direction;	これ、ここ	ぎんこうは こちらです。
32.	そちら	【N】	that way/direction;	それ、そこ	ロビーは そちらです。
33.	あちら	【N】	that way/direction;	あれ、あそこ	えきは あちらです。
34.	どちら	【N】	which way/direction;	どれ、どこ	おたくは どちらですか。

35.	みちこ	【N】	Michiko [FEMALE GIVEN NAME]	
36.	やまぐち	【N】	Yamaguchi [SURNAME]	
37.	さいとう	【N】	Saito [SURNAME]	
38.	いつ	【N,Ad】	when [QW]	みちこさんに いつ あいますか。
39.	いくつ	【N,Ad】	how many [QW]	たまごは いくつ ありますか。
40.	ちょっと	【Ad】	a bit; a little [MORE COLLOQUIAL THAN sukoshi]	ちょっと べんきょう しました。
41.	たいへん + ADJ/ADV	【Ad】	very; extremely [Opp. sukoshi]	たいへん いそがしいです。 cf. すこし いそがしいです。
42.	どうも	【Ad】	indeed; somehow	どうも ありがとう ございます。
43.	どうぞ	【Ad】	please (go ahead/accept it) [FOR GIVING PERMISSION OR OFFERING SOMETHING]	A: いいですか。 B: ええ、どうぞ。
44.	また	【Ad】	again [cf. mada "still; (not) yet"]	あした また きます。
*45.	ゆっくり	【Ad】	slowly	ゆっくり はなします。
*46.	おもしろい	【i-A】	interesting	この しょうせつは おもしろいです。
47.	つまらない	【i-A】	uninteresting; bored; trivial; worthless	あの えいがは つまらないです。
48.	～ごはん	【N】	...meal	あさごはん、ひるごはん、ばんごはん
49.	～げつ	【Suf】	...month	せんげつ、こんげつ、らいげつ
50.	そして	【Conj】	and; (and) then	うちへ かえります。 そして、すこし ねます。

Expressions:

1. おねがい します。   "Excuse me!" [IN A STORE] [ALSO, "Thank you in advance."]

2. なにを さしあげましょう(か)。   "What would you like?"

3. ごめんください。   "Hello!" [TO GET ATTENTION AT A STORE, ANOTHER'S HOUSE, ETC.]

4. おじゃま します。   "I'll (humbly) come in." [AT ANOTHER'S HOUSE, ROOM, ETC.]

5. おじゃま しました。   "I'm sorry to have bothered you." [WHEN LEAVING ANOTHER'S HOUSE, ETC.]

6. これ、つまらない ものですが、どうぞ。   "This is nothing much, but please accept it."

7. どうも すみません。   "Thank you very much (for your trouble)." "I am very sorry."

8. どうぞ おかまいなく。   "Please don't bother." "Please don't go to the trouble."

9. ありがとう ございました。   "Thank you (for what you <u>have</u> <u>done</u> for me)."

10. この〜 (e.g., かさ)、どうも ありがとう ございました。   "Thank you very much for the use of this... (e.g., umbrella)."

Numbers and Counters:

(A) 〜つ: round or chunky objects and things with no specific shape -- apples, eggs, cabbages, desks, balls, rooms, schools, <u>kanji</u>

This is the general way of counting things. This Japanese number series goes only up to ten. For numbers exceeding ten, switch to the Chinese series -- <u>juu-ichi</u>, <u>juu-ni</u>... (Note that <u>-tsu</u> is not used for numbers ten and greater.) cf. days of the month (L.5)

1: ひとつ   2: ふたつ   3: みっつ   4: よっつ   5: いつつ   6: むっつ

7: ななつ   8: やっつ   9: ここのつ   10: とお ...   いくつ "how many"

(B) 〜かげつ: ...months

1: いっかげつ   2: にかげつ   3: さんかげつ ...   なんかげつ "how many months"

Translation of the Examples:

1. I listen to records.
   I ask my teacher.
2. I use a pen.
3. I'll wait for my friend.
4. I'll wrap the box.
5. I'll invite Mr./Ms. Suzuki.
6. The cat died.
7. Are you in a hurry?
8. The child stood up.
9. Dictionaries are helpful.
10. I'll try my best.
11. You saved me! [Lit. I was saved.]
12. I'll get up on the chair.
13. I enter the classroom.
    The tea is ready!
14. I'll put the book inside my bag.
    I'll make tea.
15. I'll put a ribbon on the box.
    I turned on the television.
16. I'll give my friend a book.
17. I'll give it to my teacher.
18. I answer questions.
Rev. I left immediately.
19. I eat an apple every day.
20. This tangerine is delicious.
21. Melons are expensive.
22. There is a fruit store.
23. It's a pretty ribbon, isn't it?
24. In the morning I listen to the radio.
25. I listen to the Japanese (language) tape.
26. I listened to the tape in the language lab.
27. I bought a subway ticket.
28. I read reference books.
29. I went to my teacher's house.
30. We play baseball in the park.
31. The bank is this way.
32. The lobby is that way.
33. The station is that way [far away].
34. Where is your home? [POLITE]   OR   Which direction is it to your home?
38. When will you see Michiko?
39. How many eggs are there?
40. I studied a little.
41. I am very busy.
cf. I am a little busy.
42. Thank you <u>very</u> <u>much</u>.

43. A: Is it o.k.? (OR May I?)
    B: Yes, please (go ahead).
44. I'll come again tomorrow.
45. I speak slowly.
46. This novel is interesting.
47. That movie is boring.
48. breakfast, lunch, supper/dinner
49. last month, this month, next month
50. I'll go home. And (then) I'll sleep for a little while.

Lesson 7: Grammar

I. The -te Form of Verbs

The basic meaning of the -te form of verbs is "...and," as is the case with adjectives and the copula; it links the verb with another verb or a predicate.

(A) Formation

The -te form of verbs is constructed differently according to the groups of the verbs in their dictionary forms. In the case of u-verbs, the final syllable determines the form. For ru-verbs, drop the final -ru and add -te.

u-Verbs:

Final Syl.	-te Form	Example	Other Examples with the Same Final Syl.
-す	-して	はなす → はなして	
-く	-いて	きく → きいて	
	EXCEPTION:	いく → いって	
-ぐ	-いで	いそぐ → いそいで	
-う	-って	かう → かって	あう、つかう、ちがう
-つ		まつ → まって	たつ
-る		かえる → かえって	ある、やる、わかる、たすかる、あがる、はじまる、おわる、がんばる、ふる、はいる
-む	-んで	よむ → よんで	のむ
-ぶ		よぶ → よんで	
-ぬ		しぬ → しんで	NO OTHER VERB ENDS IN -nu

ru-Verbs:

-iru	DROP -る & ADD -て	みる → みて	いる、おきる、たりる
-eru		たべる → たべて	ねる、でかける、つける、いれる、あげる、さしあげる、こたえる

Irregular Verbs:

くる →	きて	
する →	して	べんきょうを〜、しごとを〜、スポーツを〜

(B) VERB-te kudasai   "Please do..." [REQUEST]

One of the uses of the -te form of verbs is to indicate "request" when combined with kudasai. While NOUN o kudasai means "Please give me (SOMETHING)," VERB-te kudasai is used to ask someone TO DO something; literally, "Please give me the favor of doing..."

The expression is also used to offer something or to give someone permission to do something, in which case, <u>doozo</u> is often added at the beginning to show one's eagerness and sincerity.

1. ほんを <u>かって</u> <u>ください</u>。(←かう)　　"Please buy the book."
　　　　　　　　　　　　　　　　　　　　　OR "Please buy the book <u>for</u> <u>me</u>."

2. どうぞ コーヒーを <u>のんで</u> <u>ください</u>。(←のむ)　"Please <u>do</u> help yourself to the coffee."

IN THE CLASSROOM:

3. もう いちど <u>いって</u> <u>ください</u>。　(←いう)　"Please say it one more time." (L.1)
4. しゅくだいを <u>だして</u> <u>ください</u>。　(←だす)　"Please turn in your homework."(L.2)
5. ほんを <u>よんで</u> <u>ください</u>。　　　(←よむ)　"Please read the book."
6. しつもんに <u>こたえて</u> <u>ください</u>。(←こたえる) "Please answer the question."
7. スミスさんに <u>きいて</u> <u>ください</u>。　(←きく)　"Please ask Mr./Ms. Smith."
8. ラボで テープを <u>きいて</u> <u>ください</u>。(←きく)　"Please listen to the tape in the language lab."

(C) CLAUSE (X)-te, CLAUSE (Y)　　"X, and (then) Y."

Another function of the <u>-te</u> form is to connect clauses and indicate two (or more) actions occurring in a sequence. Remember that the <u>-te</u> form does not take tense and that the tense is indicated by the final clause.

9. りょうへ <u>かえって</u>、テレビを みます。　"I'll go back to the dormitory, and
　　(←かえる)　　　　　　　　　　　　　　　watch TV." [IN ONE SENTENCE]

cf. りょうへ かえります。<u>そして</u>、テレビ　"I'll go back to the dormitory. Then
　　を みます。　　　　　　　　　　　　　　I'll watch TV." [TWO SENTENCES]

10. きのう くだものを <u>かって</u>、びょういん　"I bought some fruit, and went to the
　　へ いきました。　(←かう)　　　　　　　hospital (to visit someone) yesterday."

II. VERB (STEM)-mashoo(ka)

The "stem" of a verb is the <u>-masu</u> form of a verb minus <u>-masu</u>, e.g., <u>iki</u> for the verb <u>ikimasu</u>, "to go."

(A) ～ましょう　"Let's do..." [WHEN INVITING/URGING SOMEONE TO DO SOMETHING]

1. やきゅうを <u>やりましょう</u>。　　　　　　　"Let's play baseball."

2. A: どこかで ごはんを <u>たべましょう</u>。　　"Let's have dinner somewhere."
　 B: ええ、そう <u>しましょう</u>。　　　　　　"Yes, let's do that."

3. A: こんばんは しんじゅくへ いって、ビールを　　"Let's go to Shinjuku and drink
　　 のみましょう。　　　（←いく）　　　　　　beer tonight."
   B: ええ、いいですね。　　　　　　　　　　　　"Yes, good idea!"

(B) ～ましょうか　　"Shall we do...?" "Shall I do... (for you)?" [SUGGESTION]

    Whether an action is to be carried out by the speaker alone or jointly with the listener is determined by the context. When a question word is present in a sentence, the particle ka is optional after -mashoo.

4. A: しずかな ところへ いきましょうか。　　　"Shall we go to a quiet place?"
   B: ええ、いきましょう。　　　　　　　　　　"Yes, let's."

5. A: ゆうびんきょくへ いきましょうか。　　　"Shall I go to the post office
　　　　　　　　　　　　　　　　　　　　　　for you?"
   B: ええ、すみませんが、いって ください。　"Yes, I'm sorry (to trouble you),
　　　　　　　　　　　　　　　　　　　　　　but please (go)."

6. STORE CLERK: なに を さしあげましょう(か)。　"May I help you?" Lit. "What
　　　　　　　　　　　　　　　　　　　　　　shall I humbly give you?"
   CUSTOMER:　　その あかい さかなを ください。　"I would like that red fish."
　　　　　　　　　　　　　　　　　　　　　　Lit. "Please give me..."

III. NOUN/ADJ-deshoo(ka)

(A) ～でしょう　　"probably..." [SUPPOSITION]

    -Deshoo indicates the speaker's "supposition/conjecture," but it cannot be used with respect to the speaker himself. For example, (Watashi wa) ashita himadeshoo, "I'll probably be free tomorrow," sounds strange.

    Be sure to distinguish the pronunciation of -deshoo with that of -desu yo. Also, remember that -deshoo, like -mashoo and -te kudasai, must be attached to something and cannot stand by itself.

1. あの ひとは アメリカじんでしょう。　　　"He is probably American."
cf. あの ひとは アメリカじんですよ。　　　 "He is American, I'm telling you!"

2. この にくは あたらしいでしょう。　　　　"This meat is probably fresh."
cf. この にくは あたらしいですよ。　　　　 "This meat is fresh, I assure you!"

(B) ～でしょうか　　"Would (it) be...?" "Do you suppose...?" "I wonder..."

    -Deshoo ka is a more roundabout and, therefore, politer way of asking questions than -desu ka. Again, the particle ka is optional if there is a question word in the sentence.

3. A: やましたさんの ごしゅじんは おげんき
    でしょうか。
   B: ええ、おげんきですよ。

   "Do you suppose Mrs. Yamashita's husband is well?"
   "Yes, he is."

4. A: どこかで えいがを みましょう。
   B: ええ、でも、どこ が いいでしょう(か)。
   A: しんじゅく が いいでしょう。

   "Let's see a movie somewhere."
   "Yes, but where would be good?"
   "Shinjuku would probably be good."

Notice that in Example 4 doko (Lit. "which place") is followed by the particle ga because it is the subject and because a question word cannot be followed by wa. The answer Shinjuku, too, must take ga in such a case.

IV. QW + 'de mo' (...AFF.)   "No matter... it is" "any... (is o.k., etc.)"

	QW	QW か	QW(P) も... Neg.	QW(P) でも... Aff.
なに/なん	what	something	nothing	anything; no matter what
だれ	who	someone	no one	anyone; no matter who
どこ	where	somewhere	nowhere	anywhere; no matter where
いつ	when	sometime	-------	any time; no matter when

1. A: なにか かいましょうか。
   B: ええ、でも、なにが いいでしょうか。
   A: なんでも いいです。

   "Shall we buy something?"
   "Yes, but what would be good?"
   "Anything will be fine." Lit.
   "No matter what it is, it's o.k."

2. A: この じしょ、ありがとう ございました。
   B: どう いたしまして。
      また いつでも つかって ください。

   "Thank you for (the use of) this dictionary."
   "You're welcome.
   Please use it again any time."

V. CLAUSE (X) kara, CLAUSE (Y)   "X, so Y." "Y because X." "Since X, Y."

Kara is a conjunctive particle indicating "reason." Unlike the English word "because," it comes AFTER the reason clause. The order within a sentence must be as follows: [REASON kara,] RESULT.

1. きのうは やすみでしたから、
   いちにちじゅう うちに いました。

   "Yesterday was a holiday, so I stayed home all day." OR "I stayed home... because..."

2. あしたは テストが ありますから、
   がんばって ください。

   "There is a test tomorrow, so please try your best (OR I wish you good luck)."

In speech, though not in writing, the order of the two clauses is often reversed. Instead of "X kara, Y," you could say, "Y. X kara." Note that the particle kara is still attached to the reason clause.

3. a. きっぷを かいますから、ちょっと まって ください。 "I'm going to buy the ticket, so please wait for a moment."
   b. ちょっと まって ください。きっぷを かいますから。 "Please wait for a moment. I'm going to buy the ticket, so..."

VI. Numbers and Counters   cf. p.46

1. Q: この だいがくに としょかんが いくつ ありますか。 (OR は) "How many libraries are there in this university?"
   A: みっつ あります。 "There are three."

2. その りんごを とお ください。 "Please give me ten of those apples."

3. いっしゅうかんに かんじを じゅうごぐらい べんきょう します。 "We study about fifteen kanji a week."

4. Q: ニューヨークに どのぐらい いましたか。 "How long were you in New York?"
   A: いっかげつぐらいです。 "About a month."

VII. 'Taihen' vs. 'Sukoshi' "very" vs. "a little"

The word taihen, which we learned earlier, is a na-type adjective meaning "tough." Another use of this word is as an adverb indicating a degree, "very." While sukoshi "a few; a little" and amari "(not) many/much; (not) very" can be used for both an amount and a degree, you must say takusan, and not taihen, when referring to an amount.

1. a. アパートは たいへん たかいです。 "The apartment is very expensive."
   b. アパートは すこし たかいです。 "The apartment is a little expensive."
   c. アパートは あまり たかく ありません。 "The apartment isn't very (OR so) expensive."

2. a. たいへん おそく かえりました。 "I went home very late."
   b. すこし おそく かえりました。 "I went home a little late."
   c. あまり おそく かえりませんでした。 "I didn't go home very (OR so) late."

3. a. こどもは たくさん います。 "There are many children."
   b. こどもは すこし います。 "There are a few (OR some) children."
   c. こどもは あまり いません。 "There aren't (that) many children."

Lesson 8 (だいはっか): New Vocabulary

1.	NOUN で	【P】	by; with; in; using... [MEANS/INSTRUMENT]	にほんご<u>で</u> はなします。
*2.	PERSON と	【P】	with... [PARTNER]	ともだち<u>と</u> でかけます。
*3.	PLACE に	【P】	on(to); in(to)... [DESTINATION]	きょうしつ<u>に</u> はいりました。
4.	VERB(STEM) に + MOTION VERB	【P】	(in order) to do...; for (the purpose of) doing..." [PURPOSE]	ほんを よみ<u>に</u> いきました。
5.	(Xに) すむ すんで いる [STATE]	【u-V】	will live; reside (in X) to live; be living (in X)	とうきょうに すんで います。
6.	(Xに) つとめる つとめて いる [STATE]	【ru-V】	will be employed (at X) to be employed (at X)	ぎんこうに つとめて います。
7.	(Xを) もつ もって いる [STATE]	【u-V】	to hold to have; own; possess	うちを もって います。
8.	(Xを) きる きて いる [STATE]	【ru-V】	to put on; wear X to have X on; be wearing X	くろい ふくを きて います。
9.	(Xに Yを) かく	【u-V】	to write (Y on X)	かみに なまえを かきました。
*10.	あるく	【u-V】	to walk	ここへ あるいて きました。
11.	あそぶ	【u-V】	to play (around); goof off	いちにちじゅう あそびます。
12.	(Xに Yを) うる	【u-V】	to sell (Y to X)	ともだちに ほんを うります。
*13.	(Xに Yを) おしえる	【ru-V】	to teach (Y to X); to tell (X Y)	こどもに すいえいを おしえます。
14.	(でんわを) かける	【ru-V】	to call (on the phone)	こんばん でんわを かけます。
15.	でんわ	【VN,N】	telephone	こんばん でんわを します。
16.	けっこん (Xと) けっこん する 〜 して いる [STATE]	【VN】	marriage to marry X to be married	らいげつ けっこん します。 もう けっこん して います。
17.	ぼうえき ぼうえき がいしゃ	【VN】 【N】	trade; trading trading company	にほんと ぼうえきを します。
18.	せんもん	【N】	major (field of study); specialty	せんもんは なんですか。
19.	けいざい(がく)	【N】	economics [keezai ALONE COULD MEAN "economy"]	せんもんは けいざいです。
20.	せいじ(がく)	【N】	political science [seeji ALONE COULD MEAN "politics"]	せいじは おもしろいです。

21.	かがく	【N】	science	かがくの テストが あります。
22.	いがく	【N】	medical science	いがくを べんきょう します。
23.	ぶんがく	【N】	literature	たいてい ぶんがくを よみます。
24.	れきし	【N】	history	れきしの ほんを かいました。
25.	えいご	【N】	English (language)	えいごで はなしました。
26.	イギリス (OR えいこく)	【N】	England; Great Britain [Eekoku SOUNDS BOOKISH]	イギリスへ いきました。
27.	フランス	【N】	France	フランスじんと けっこん します。
28.	ドイツ	【N】	Germany	ドイツで ともだちに あいました。
29.	ロシア	【N】	Russia	せんもんは ロシアごです。
30.	きゃく	【N】	guest; visitor; customer	あした おきゃくさんが きます。
31.	へや	【N】	room	へやは たいへん ひろいです。
32.	やくしょ	【N】	government office	やくしょに つとめて います。
33.	めいし	【N】	business card	めいしを さしあげましょうか。
34.	ばんごう	【N】	number	へやの ばんごうが わかりません。
	でんわ ばんごう	【N】	telephone number	でんわ ばんごうを ききました。
*35.	じゅうしょ	【N】	address	じゅうしょを かいて ください。
36.	おかね	【N】	money	おかねを すこし もって います。
37.	ふく	【N】	clothes	あたらしい ふくを きて います。
38.	きかい	【N】	machine	おおきくて たかい きかいです。
39.	ひこうき	【N】	airplane	ひこうきは はやいですね。
*40.	くるま	【N】	car	くるまで いきましょう。
*41.	バス	【N】	bus	バスが あります。
42.	れい (OR ゼロ)	【N】	zero	ばんごうは よんれいはちです。
43.	こちら	【N】	[POLITE FOR -- kono hito "this person"] こちらは なかむらせんせいです。	
44.	かわかみ	【N】	Kawakami [SURNAME]	
45.	ジョンソン	【N】	Johnson	
46.	ぎんざ	【N】	Ginza [PLACE NAME]	
47.	なかの	【N】	Nakano [PLACE NAME]	
48.	こんど	【N,Ad】	this time; next time; sometime soon	こんど うちへ きて ください。
49.	きょねん	【N,Ad】	last year	きょねん だいがくに はいりました。
50.	さっき	【N,Ad】	a little while ago; a couple of minutes ago	みちこさんは さっき かえりました。

51. あとで	【Ad】	later [ato + de]		じゃ、また あとで きます。
52. こまかい (おかね)	【i-A】	small (change)		こまかい おかねを もって います。
53. わかい	【i-A】	young		あの ひとは まだ わかいです。
54. もしもし	【Int】	Hello. [FOR TELEPHONE CONVERSATION]		
55. さあ	【Conj】	Gee...; Well... [IMPLIES LACK OF KNOWLEDGE]		
				さあ、わかりません。

Expressions:

a. はじめまして。　　　　　　　　"How do you do." Lit. "for the first time"
b. どうぞ よろしく。　　　　　　"I'm glad to meet you." Lit. "Please be good."
c. そうですね。　　　　　　　　　"Well..." "Let me think..." "Let me see..."
d. ...さんを おねがいします。　　"Mr./Ms. ---, please." [TELEPHONE CONVERSATION]

Numbers and Counters:

〜ばん: number...

1: いちばん　　2: にばん　　3: さんばん　　4: よんばん...　　なんばん "what number"

Translation of the Examples:

1. We speak in Japanese.
2. I go out with my friends.
3. I entered the classroom.
4. I went (in order) to read books.
5. I live in Tokyo.
6. I am employed at a bank.
7. I own a house.
8. He/She has black clothes on.
9. I wrote my name on the paper.
10. I walked here. [Lit. I walked and came here.]
11. I'll play all day.
12. I'll sell the book to my friend.
13. I teach children how to swim (Lit. swimming).
14. I'll give you a call tonight.
15. I'll give you a call tonight.
16. I'm getting married next month.
    He/She is already married.
17. We trade with Japan.
18. What is your major?
19. My major is economics.

20. Politics is interesting.
21. I have a science test.
22. I'll study medical science.
23. I usually read literature.
24. I bought a history book.
25. We spoke in English.
26. I went to England (OR Great Britain).
27. I'm marrying a French person.
28. I saw my friend in Germany.
29. My major is Russian language.
30. The guests are coming tomorrow.
31. The room is very spacious.
32. I work for (OR am employed at) a government office.
33. Shall I (humbly) give you my card?
34. I don't know the room number.
    I asked the phone number.
35. Please write your address.
36. I have a little money.
37. He/She is wearing new clothes.
38. It's a big and expensive machine.
39. Airplanes are fast, aren't they.
40. Let's go by car.
41. There is a bus.
42. The number is 408.
43. This gentleman (OR lady) is Prof. Nakamura.
48. Please come over to my house next time (OR sometime soon).
49. I entered the university last year.
50. Michiko left (Lit. returned; went home) just a while ago.
51. Then I'll come again later.
52. I have some small change.
53. He/She (Lit. That person) is still young.
55. Gee, I don't know.

Lesson 8: Grammar

I. VERB-te imasu

In this pattern iru/imasu functions as an auxiliary verb, and it is used whether the subject of the main verb is animate (people and animals) or inanimate (things and events).

The affirmative-negative and present-past distinctions are expressed by changing imasu in appropriate forms. In response to a question which ends with ...te imasu ka, you must repeat the main verb, and not just imasu.

(A) Action in Progress   "is doing..." (sometimes "will be/has been doing")

1. たなかさんは いま ほんを よんで います。   "Mr. Tanaka is reading a book now."
   [ACTION IN PROGRESS]

cf. たなかさんは ほんを よみます。   "Mr. Tanaka reads (OR will read) books." [HABITUAL OR FUTURE ACTION]

2. a. Pres. Aff.: ねて います。   "He is sleeping."
   b. Pres. Neg.: ねて いません。   "He is not sleeping."
   c. Past Aff.: ねて いました。   "He was sleeping."
   d. Past Neg.: ねて いませんでした。   "He was not sleeping."

3. Q: あめが ふって いますか。   "Is it raining?"
   A: いいえ、ふって いません。   "No, it isn't."

4. Q: みちこさんは いま なにを して いますか。   "What is Michiko doing now?"
   A: ラジオを きいて います。   "She is listening to the radio."

5. Q: きのうの よる じゅうじごろ なにを して いましたか。   "What were you doing around ten o'clock last (yesterday's) night?"
   A: なにも して いませんでした。   "I wasn't doing anything."

(B) Resultant State   "has done... (AND THE RESULT REMAINS UNCHANGED)"

With all motion verbs such as iku "go" and kuru "come" as well as with change-of-state verbs, the ...te imasu pattern expresses the state resulting from an action. "Change-of-state" verbs such as okiru "get up" and shinu "die" express actions or events before and after which the state is different. While the focus is on whether an action has been completed or not with the ...mashita form, the focus with ...te imasu is on the continuing state.

This pattern will be discussed in more detail in Lesson 18. It will be helpful for now to memorize the sentences which commonly appear in the pattern, such as listed below.

6. ともだちは うちへ き<u>て</u> <u>います</u>。	"My friend has come to my house (and he is still at my house)."
cf. ともだちは うちへ きます。	"My friend is coming (will come) to my house."
7. ニューヨークに すん<u>で</u> <u>います</u>。	"He/She lives in New York."
cf. ニューヨークに すみます。	"He/She will live in New York."
8. スミスさんは けっこん し<u>て</u> <u>います</u>。	"Mr./Ms. Smith is married."
cf. スミスさんは けっこん します。	"Mr./Ms. Smith will get married."
9. きょうは あかい ふくを き<u>て</u> <u>います</u>。	"She's wearing a red dress today."
cf. きょうは あかい ふくを きます。	"She will put on a red dress today."
10. この いぬは しん<u>で</u> <u>います</u>よ。	"This dog is dead (and it's here)!"
cf. この いぬは しにますよ。	"This dog is dying (will die)!"

QUESTION: How do you say: (1) "Mr. Tanaka has gone out (and he is still out)" and (2) "Mr. Tanaka is going out tonight" in Japanese?

II. VERB (STEM) ni + Motion Verb   "go (come, return, etc.) in order to do..."

The verb "stem" is obtained by dropping -<u>masu</u> from a verb in its -<u>masu</u> form. The stem itself does not carry tense; the tense is indicated at the end of a sentence. The particle <u>ni</u> here indicates "purpose." Remember that this purpose construction functions with motion verbs only.

1. Q: としょかんへ なにを し<u>に</u> いきますか。	"What do you go to the library <u>for</u>?"
A: ざっしを よみ<u>に</u> いきます。	Lit. "You go to the library <u>to</u> do what?" "I go there <u>to</u> read magazines."
2. Q: どこへ くつを かい<u>に</u> いきますか。	"Where do you go <u>to</u> buy shoes?"
A: しんじゅくの みせへ いきます。	"I go to the stores in Shinjuku."
3. A: あした どこかへ のみ<u>に</u> いきましょう。	"Let's go somewhere <u>to</u> drink tomorrow."
B: ええ、そう しましょう。	"Yes, let's do that."
4. こんど うちへ あそび<u>に</u> き<u>て</u> ください。	"Please come to my house for a visit (Lit. <u>to</u> play) sometime soon."
5. きのう しごとの あと ホテルの しょくどう に ごはんを たべ<u>に</u> はいりました。	"Yesterday after work I went into the hotel restaurant to eat."

III. Particles 'de,' 'to' and 'ni'

X (THING) <u>de</u> means "by (means of) X; with X; using X." X (PERSON) <u>to</u> means "with X (someone)."

1. Q: なんで がっこうへ いきますか。　　"How (By what means) do you go to school?"
   A1: バスで いきます。　　　　　　　　　"I go by bus."
   A2: あるいて いきます。　　　　　　　　"I walk (and go)." OR "I go on foot."

2. Q: きのうは だれと でかけましたか。　　"Whom did you go out with yesterday?"
   A: さとうさんと でかけました。　　　　"I went out with Mr./Ms. Sato."

3. a. ペンで なまえを かきました。　　　"I wrote my name with a pen."
   b. かたかなで なまえを かきました。　"I wrote my name in katakana."

4. ときどき ともだちと にほんごで はなします。 "I sometimes speak in Japanese with my friend."

The particle ni for place of existence is also used with sunde iru "to live/reside" and tsutomete iru "to be employed." Give the larger area first with no, and then the smaller area when you give your address in Japanese.

5. Q: どこに すんで いますか。　　　　　　"Where do you live?"
   A: とうきょうの なかのに すんで います。 "I live in Nakano, Tokyo."

6. いま かいしゃに つとめて います。　　"He is employed at a company now." [STATE]

cf. いま かいしゃで しごとを して います。 "He is working at the office now." [ACTION IN PROGRESS]

IV. CLAUSE (X) no de, CLAUSE (Y)　　"X, so Y." "Y because X." "Since X, Y."

No de is a conjunctive particle indicating "reason." While it sounds more reserved and polite than kara, they are often interchangeable. No de, however, is best used when the result clause is a factual statement. If that clause contains endings that involve speaker's or listener's volition or intention, such as ...te kudasai and ...mashoo(ka), kara should be used.

1. きのうは あめが ふりましたので (OR から)、   "It rained yesterday, so I
   どこへも いきませんでした。   didn't go anywhere." OR "I
                                              didn't go anywhere because..."

cf. a. おちゃを いれますから、ちょっと まって ください。(NOT ので)
    b. いい てんきですから、こうえんへ いきましょうか。(NOT ので)

The clause order can be reversed in speech, as shown in the following example.

2. すみませんが、きょうは はやく しつれい   "I'm sorry, but I'm leaving early to-
   します。きゃくが きますので。   day. I'm having some guests, so..."

V. Prefixes 'o-' and 'go-'

The prefixes o- and go- indicate "politeness" toward the listener or the person referred to. Generally, you do not use either one referring to your own (or your family's) belongings, although some words cannot be used without one, e.g., go-han. Also, the meanings sometimes differ according to their presence or absence, such as go-shujin "someone else's husband" and shujin "my husband." Women tend to use these prefixes more often than men.

O- is attached mainly to words of Japanese origin, while go- is always attached to words of Chinese origin. Loan words from the West usually do not take either one (but if anything, o-). Go- can only be prefixed to nouns, but o- can appear before nouns, adjectives and verb stems. Since not all words take these prefixes, you must learn the usage case by case.

With nouns: おなまえ、おかね、おちゃ、おてんき、ごはん、ごしゅじん...

With adjectives:

1. A: おげんきですか。　　　　　　　　　"Are you well?"
   B: ええ、げんきです。(NOT お FOR ONESELF)　"Yes, I'm fine."

2. A: ごしゅじんは おわかいですね。　　"Your husband looks young, doesn't he?"
   B: え？ いつ しゅじんに あいましたか。"Pardon? When did you meet my husband?"

VI. The Particle 'mo' "too; also" "either; neither" [in negative sentences]

1. A: きょうは いい てんきですね。
   B: ええ、あしたも いい てんきでしょう。

2. Reading Comprehension (L.6, p.66):
   まつもとさんの うちは おおきくて りっぱな うちでした。
   おくさんも きれいな ひとでした。[ANOTHER POSITIVE FEATURE]

3. やましたさんは がくせいじゃ ありません。　"Mr. Yamashita is not a student."
   さとうさんも がくせいじゃ ありません。　"Mr. Sato is not a student, either."

4. わたしの アパートは ひろく ありません。　"My apartment is not spacious."
   さとうさんの アパートも ひろく ありません。"Neither is Mr. Sato's apartment."

5. Reading Comprehension (L.8, p.93):
   (うちは) えきの そばですから、しずかじゃ　"(My house) is close to the station,
   ありません。　　　　　　　　　　　　　　so it's not quiet."

   へやも ひろく ありません。　　　　　　　"The rooms aren't big, either."
   　　　　　　　　　　　　　　　　　　　　[ANOTHER NEGATIVE FEATURE]

Lesson 9 (だいきゅうか): New Vocabulary

1. CLAUSE と 【P】 that... [QUOTATION]
2. Xと いう Y 【PPhr】 Y called X; 「こころ」と いう ほんを よみます。
   /yuu/ Y by the name of X
3. PLACE を 【P】 [PLACE OF MOTION] こうえんを あるきます。
4. (Xを) でる 【ru-V】 to get out of; leave X くじに うちを でました。
   [Opp. X ni hairu]
5. (Xと) いう 【u-V】 to say (that X) これは たかいと いいました。
6. (Xと) おもう 【u-V】 to think (that X) これは たかいと おもいます。
7. (Xを) かける 【ru-V】 to put on; wear (glasses)
   かけて いる [STATE] to have (glasses) on めがねを かけて います。
*8. (Xを) はく 【u-V】 to put on; wear (shoes, socks, slacks, etc.)
   はいて いる [STATE] to have (shoes, etc.) on くつを はいて いませんね。
9. (Xを) しる 【u-V】 to get to know; to find out about X
   しって いる [STATE] to know; to be familiar with X
   A: みちこさんを しって いますか。
   B: いいえ、しりません。
10. やせる 【ru-V】 to get thin; slim down
    やせて いる [STATE] to be thin おくさんは やせて います。
11. ふとる 【u-V】 to get fat; gain weight
    ふとって いる [STATE] to be fat ごしゅじんは ふとって います。
12. せい 【N】 (person's) height もりさんは せいが たかいです。
13. めがね 【N】 (eye) glasses これは あたらしい めがねです。
14. かお 【N】 face かおが あかいですね。
15. よう 【N】 errand; something to attend to きょうは ようが あります。
16. ばいてん 【N】 (news)stand ばいてんで ざっしを かいます。
17. せんぱい 【N】 one's senior こうこうの せんぱいです。
18. こうはい 【N】 one's junior [Opp. senpai] こうはいに しごとを おしえます。
19. ミラー 【N】 Miller
*20. ボストン 【N】 Boston
*21. シカゴ 【N】 Chicago
*22. ロサンゼルス 【N】 Los Angeles
*23. ワシントン 【N】 Washington
*24. ロンドン 【N】 London
*25. モスクワ 【N】 Moscow
*26. パリ 【N】 Paris

27.	けさ	【N,Ad】 this morning	けさ はやく おきました。
28.	このあいだ	【N,Ad】 the other day; recently	このあいだ けっこん しました。
29.	だめ(な)	【na-A】 no good; hopeless; spoiled	あしたは だめです。
30.	ひくい	【i-A】 low [Opp. takai]	よしださんは せいが ひくいです。
*31.	せまい	【i-A】 narrow; small space [Opp. hiroi]	アパートは せまいです。
32.	ない	【i-A】 not; non-existent [PLAIN NEGATIVE WORD]	
33.	もう + AMOUNT	【Ad】 ...more	もう すこし まちましょうか。

Expressions:

a. おそく なって すみません。   "I'm sorry I'm late."
　　　　　　　　　　　　　　　　Lit. "I have become late and I'm sorry."

b. わかりました。   "Now I know." "I got it."

Translation of the Examples:

2. I'll read a book called "The Heart of Things."
3. I'll walk around the park.
4. I left my house at nine o'clock.
5. He/She said that this is expensive.
6. I think that this is expensive.
7. He/She wears glasses.
8. He isn't wearing shoes, is he?
9. A: Do you know (of) Michiko? B: No, I don't.
10. His wife is thin.
11. Her husband is fat.
12. Mr. Mori is tall.
13. These are my new glasses.
14. His/Her face is red, isn't it?
15. I have an errand to run today.
16. I'll buy a magazine at the newsstand.
17. He was ahead of me at high school.
18. I teach (how to do) the job to the junior people.
27. I got up early this morning.
28. I got married recently.
29. Tomorrow is no good. OR I can't make it tomorrow.
30. Mr. Yoshida is short.
31. My apartment is small.
33. Shall we wait a little more?

Lesson 9: Grammar

I. The Plain Form

In the polite speech, the -desu/-masu form is used at the end of a sentence, while the "plain" form is used within a sentence, i.e., at the end of a subordinate clause. There are distinctions of tenses and affirmative and negative in the plain form just as in the -desu/-masu form. (The "dictionary" form is the plain present affirmative form.) In this lesson we will learn the plain form in the present tense only, and in the following contexts:

(1) preceding to omoimasu "(I) think that..."
(2) preceding to itte imashita "(he/she) said that..."
(3) preceding deshoo "probably..."
(4) preceding a noun, as in noun modification

Note that nai "not; non-existent" is the plain form counterpart of arimasen, and it appears in all the negative forms.

(A) I-Type Adjectives in the Present Tense

	Affirmative	Negative
Polite	やすいです	やすく ありません
Plain	やすい	やすく ない

	Affirmative	Negative
Polite	いいです	よく ありません
Plain	いい	よく ない

(B) The Copula (desu) in the Present Tense

With a na-type adjective:

	Affirmative	Negative
Polite	しずかです	しずかじゃ ありません
Plain	しずかだ	しずかじゃ ない

With a noun:

	Affimative	Negative
Polite	こどもです	こどもじゃ ありません
Plain	こどもだ	こどもじゃ ない

(C) Verbs in the Present Tense

u-Verbs:

Polite Aff. ...i-masu	Plain Aff. ...u	Plain Neg. ...a-nai
はなします	はなす	はなさない
かきます	かく	かかない
いそぎます	いそぐ	いそがない
あいます	あう	あわない
まちます	まつ	またない
ふります	ふる	ふらない
よみます	よむ	よまない
あそびます	あそぶ	あそばない
しにます	しぬ	しなない

EXCEPTION:

Polite Aff.	Plain Aff.	Plain Neg.
あります	ある	ない

ru-Verbs: For the plain negative form, replace the final -ru with -nai.

ねます	ねる	ねない
おきます	おきる	おきない

Irregular Verbs:

きます	くる	こない
します	する	しない

II. The Plain Form + to omoimasu   "(I) think that..."

The particle <u>to</u>, which indicates "quotation," appears after a clause ending in the plain form and before the verbs meaning "to think," "to say," "to hear," etc. Unlike the English word "that," the particle cannot be omitted.

The subject of the verb <u>omou/omoimasu</u> is either "I" or "you" (in a question), and therefore it is not specified unless the speaker wants to contrast what "I" or "you" think with someone else's thought or opinion.

The tense within a quotation is kept exactly as it is thought (or said). For example, "I <u>think</u> that it <u>is</u> expensive" and "I <u>thought</u> that it <u>was</u> expensive" (Literally: "I thought, 'it <u>is</u> expensive'") will both have the quotation in the present tense, while the main verb <u>think</u> will indicate the present or past distinction. Negation usually occurs in the clause that precedes <u>to omoimasu</u>, rather than using the negative form of <u>omoimasu</u>.

(A) With an i-type adjective:

1. さかなは おいし<u>い</u>と　　おもいます。 "I think that the fish is delicious."
2. さかなは おいし<u>く</u> ないと おもいます。 "I don't think the fish is delicious."
3. さかなは おいし<u>い</u>と　　おもいました。"I thought that the fish was delicious."
4. さかなは おいし<u>く</u> ないと おもいました。"I didn't think the fish was delicious."

(B) With a na-type adjective

5. こどもは げんき<u>だ</u>と　　おもいます。　"I think that the child is well."
6. こどもは げんき<u>じゃ</u> ないと おもいます。　"I don't think the child is well."
7. こどもは げんき<u>だ</u>と　　おもいました。　"I thought that the child was well."
8. こどもは げんき<u>じゃ</u> ないと おもいました。　"I didn't think the child was well."

(C) With a noun

9. きょうは やすみ<u>だ</u>と　　おもいます。　"I think that today is a holiday."
10. きょうは やすみ<u>じゃ</u> ないと おもいます。　"I don't think today is a holiday."
11. きょうは やすみ<u>だ</u>と　　おもいました。　"I thought that today was a holiday."
12. きょうは やすみ<u>じゃ</u> ないと おもいました。　"I didn't think today was a holiday."

(D) With a verb

13. Q: たなかさんは ほんを よ<u>む</u>と おもいますか。　"Do you think that Mr. Tanaka will read the book?"

    A: いいえ、よ<u>ま</u>ないと おもいます。　"No, I don't think he will."

14. たなかさんは ほんを よ<u>む</u>と おもいました。   "I thought that Mr. Tanaka would read the book."

15. たなかさんは ほんを よ<u>まない</u>と おもいました。   "I didn't think that Mr. Tanaka would read the book."

16. たなかさんは いま としょかんで ほんを よん<u>で</u> <u>いる</u>と おもいます。   "I think that Mr. Tanaka <u>is reading</u> books in the library now."

III. The Plain Form + to itte imashita   "(He/She) said that..."

While the direct quotation often appears in monologues, such as in essays and story telling, the indirect quotation in the plain form is much more common in conversation. Also, <u>to itte imashita</u> (Lit. "was saying that..."), rather than <u>to iimashita</u> "said that...," is frequently used in speech.

To indicate to whom an utterance is directed, use the particle <u>ni</u> for target/indirect object. <u>Watashi ni</u> "to me," however, is usually omitted.

1. Direct Quotation:
   もりさんは「ぎんこうへ <u>いきます。</u>」と いいました。   "Mr. Mori said, 'I'm going to the bank.'"

   Indirect Quotation:
   もりさんは ぎんこうへ <u>いく</u>と いって いました。   "Mr. Mori said (OR told me) that (OR いいました。)   he was going to the bank."

2. やましたさんは あした | ひま<u>だ</u> / いそがしい / くる / こない | と いって いましたよ。

   "Mr. Yamashita said that he is | free / busy / coming / not coming | tomorrow."

3. A: よしださんは まだ がくせいですか。   "Is Ms. Yoshida still a student?"
   B: いいえ、いまは としょかんに <u>つとめて</u> <u>いる</u>と いって いましたよ。   "No, she said that she is employed at the library now."

IV. The Plain Form + deshoo   "probably..." cf. L.7, III.

A clause must end in the plain form when it appears before <u>-deshoo</u>. One exception is that the copula <u>da</u> is deleted. In the case of the present affirmative form, place nouns and the stems of <u>na</u>-type adjectives directly before <u>-deshoo</u>.

1. a. すずきさんは <u>まつ</u>でしょう。　　　　　　"Mr. Suzuki will probably wait."
   b. すずきさんは <u>またない</u>でしょう。　　　　"Mr. Suzuki probably won't wait."
   c. すずきさんは <u>まって</u> <u>いる</u>でしょう。　　"Mr. Suzuki is probably waiting."
   d. すずきさんは <u>まって</u> <u>いない</u>でしょう。　"Mr. Suzuki probably isn't waiting."

2. a. あの くるまは ふる<u>い</u>でしょう。　　　　　"That car is probably old."
   b. あの くるまは あまり ふる<u>く</u> <u>ない</u>でしょう。"That car probably isn't so old."

3. a. パーティーは にぎやかでしょう。　　　　　　"The party is probably lively."
   b. パーティーは にぎやか<u>じゃ</u> <u>ない</u>でしょう。"The party probably isn't lively."

4. a. せんもんは れきしでしょう。　　　　　　　　"His major is probably history."
   b. せんもんは れきし<u>じゃ</u> <u>ない</u>でしょう。　"His major probably isn't history."

5. Q: こんばんは あめが <u>ふる</u>でしょうか。　　　"Do you suppose it'll rain tonight?"
                                                  OR "I wonder if it'll rain tonight."

   A: さあ、<u>ふらない</u>と おもいますが...　　　 "Gee, I don't think it will, but..."

   cf. こんばんは あめが ふりますか。　　　　　　"Will it rain tonight?"

V. Noun Modification

Modifiers always come BEFORE words to be modified in Japanese. Therefore, <u>nouns, adjectives and verbs must precede the noun which they modify</u>. <u>Noun modifiers also must be in the PLAIN form</u>. An exception is that the present affirmative form of the copula, <u>da</u>, cannot appear before nouns; use <u>no</u> with nouns and <u>na</u> with <u>na</u>-type adjectives. Remember that the polite (-<u>desu</u>/-<u>masu</u>) form or the -<u>te</u> form cannot modify a noun.

(A) With a noun

1. ［ にほんじん<u>の</u> ］ せんせいが います。　　"There are [Japanese] teachers." OR
                                                  "There are teachers [who are Japanese]."

2. ［ にほんじん<u>じゃ</u> <u>ない</u> ］ せんせいが　"There are [non-Japanese] teachers." OR
   います。　　　　　　　　　　　　　　　　　　　"There are teachers [who are not Japanese]."

(B) With a na-type adjective

3. りょうは ［ りっぱ<u>な</u> ］ たてものです。　"The dormitory is a [stately] building."
                                                  OR "The dormitory is a building [which is stately]."

4. りょうは ［ あまり りっぱ<u>じゃ</u> <u>ない</u> ］　"The dormitory is a building [which is
   たてものです。　　　　　　　　　　　　　　　　　not very stately]."

(C) With an i-type adjective

5. [たかい] ふくを かいます。　　"I buy [expensive] clothes." OR
　　　　　　　　　　　　　　　　　　"I buy clothes [which are expensive]."

6. [たかく ない] ふくを かいます。　"I buy [non-expensive] clothes." OR
　　　　　　　　　　　　　　　　　　"I buy clothes [which are not expensive]."

(D) With a verb

7. もりさんは [やせて いる] ひとです。　"Mr. Mori is a [thin] person." OR
　　　　　　　　　　　　　　　　　　　　"Mr. Mori is a person [who is thin]."

8. もりさんは [やせて いない] ひとです。"Mr. Mori is a person [who is not thin]."

9. Q: [あの へやで テレビを みて いる] 　"Who is the man [(who is) watching TV
　　　ひとは だれですか。　　　　　　　　　 in that room]?"

　　A: ああ、あの ひとは ジョンソンさんです。"Oh, that is Mr. Johnson."

10. Q: こばやしさんは どの ひとですか。　　"Which one is Ms. Kobayashi?"

　　A: [あそこで レコードを きいて いる] 　"She is the person [who is listening
　　　ひとです。　　　　　　　　　　　　　　 to records over there]."

11. Q: ごしゅじんは どんな ひとですか。　　"What is her husband like?"

　　A: [めがねを かけて いて、ふとって 　　"He is a person [who wears glasses
　　　いる] ひとです。　　　　　　　　　　 and is fat]."

Note that the questions in Examples 10 and 11 above are quite different. Dono hito asks the listener to point to someone among all the people present, while donna hito simply asks for a description of the person.

VI. 'Moo' and 'Mada'　cf. L.4, III.

To express that "something has not happened yet," mada ...-masen or -te imasen is used with motion verbs and change-of-state verbs, and -te imasen with other (durative) verbs. -Masen-deshita is inappropriate in this case.

1. Q: スミスさんは もう かえりましたか。　"Has Mr. Smith already returned?"
　　　　　　　　　　　　　　　　　　　　OR "Has Mr. Smith returned yet?"

　　A: いいえ、まだ かえりません。/かえって いません。"No, he hasn't returned yet."

2. まだ ひるごはんを たべて いません。　"I haven't had lunch yet."

3. Q: まだ べんきょう して いますか。　　"Are you still studying?"

　　A: いいえ、もう して いません。　　　"No, I'm not studying any more."

4. Q: おかねは もう ありませんね。　　　　"There is no more money, right?"

　　A: いいえ、まだ すこし あると おもいます。"No, I think there is still some (left)."

Lesson 10 (だい十か（じっ）): New Vocabulary

1. NOUN (X) から 【P】 from; starting X [STARTING POINT IN TIME AND SPACE]
   やすみは 十二月（じゅうにがつ） 十九日（じゅうくにち）からです。

*2. NOUN (X) まで 【P】 until; as far as X [ENDING POINT IN TIME AND SPACE]
   やすみは 一月（いちがつ） 七日（なのか）までです。

3. NOUN の 【P】 [SUBJECT WITHIN A NOUN MODIFYING CLAUSE]
   田中（たなか）さんは せいの たかい 人（ひと）です。

4. (Xと) ちがう 【u-V】 to be different (from X)
   かんこくごは 日本（にほん）ごと ちがいます。

5. (〜に/く) なる 【u-V】 to become; get; turn... おそく なって すみません。

6. (Xを) とる 【u-V】 to take X こうこうで ドイツごを とりました。

7. (Xに) すわる 【u-V】 to sit (in/on X) みちこさんの となりに すわります。

8. (Xを) ならう 【u-V】 to learn X (from someone);
   take lessons (in X) せんしゅう かんじを ならいました。

9. (Xを) もらう 【u-V】 to receive; get X おもしろい ものを もらいました。

10. (Xに Yを) みせる 【ru-V】 to show (Y to X); let X see Y
    ともだちに あたらしい ふくを みせました。

11. (Xが) できる 【ru-V】 (for X) to come out; be made ごはんが できましたよ。

12. しゃしん 【N】 photograph; picture しゃしんを とりましょうか。

13. てがみ 【N】 letter てがみを かいて ください。

14. おんがく 【N】 music よく おんがくを ききます。

15. (お)かし 【N】 sweets; snack あまり おかしを たべません。

16. (お)べんとう 【N】 box(ed) lunch 一（いち）じに おべんとうを たべます。

17. ことば 【N】 word; phrase; language いろいろな ことばを ならいます。

*18. ぶんぽう 【N】 grammar ぶんぽうも べんきょう します。

19. (お)てら 【N】 Buddhist temple ふるい おてらを みに いきます。

20. ちゃみせ 【N】 (old-fashioned) little tea house
    [cha "tea" + mise "store"] ちゃみせに はいりましょう。

21. せき 【N】 seat せきが たりません。

22. さいふ 【N】 wallet さいふが ありません。

23. おじいさん 【N】 grandfather; old man おじいさんは おげんきですか。

24. おばあさん 【N】 grandmother; old woman おばあさんと はなしました。

25.	ぼく	【N】	I [USED ONLY BY MEN IN INFORMAL SITUATIONS]	ぼくは なかむら よしおです。
*26.	クラス	【N】	class	きょうは クラスが ありません。
27.	べつ	【N】	different; separate	おかねは べつの ところです。
28.	はじめ	【N】	the first; the beginning	はじめの クラスは せいじです。
29.	つぎ	【N】	next	つぎの クラスは けいざいです。
30.	さいご	【N】	the last; the end	さいごの クラスは れきしです。
31.	はやし	【N】	Hayashi [SURNAME]	
32.	きょうと	【N】	Kyoto [PLACE NAME]	
33.	きよみずでら	【N】	Kiyomizu Temple [NAME OF A TEMPLE]	
34.	さんじゅうさんげんどう	【N】	Sanjusangendo [NAME OF A TEMPLE]	
35.	へいあん じんぐう	【N】	Heian Shrine [NAME OF A SHINTO SHRINE]	
36.	みんな	【N,Ad】	all; everyone	がくせいは みんな きました。
	みなさん		Everyone!; Ladies and gentlemen! [IN ADDRESSING, POLITE]	
37.	ゆうべ	【N,Ad】	last night	ゆうべ おそく かえりました。
38.	あかるい	【i-A】	bright; light	きょうしつは あかるいです。
39.	くらい	【i-A】	dark [Opp. akarui]	この へやは くらいですね。
40.	うるさい	【i-A】	noisy	りょうは ときどき うるさいです。
*41.	まずい	【i-A】	tastes awful [Opp. oishii]	この ステーキは まずいですね。
42.	たしか(な)	【na-A】	certain; sure	それは たしかです。
43.	ずいぶん	【Ad】	very (to a surprising degree)	ずいぶん はやいですねえ。
44.	いろいろ	【Ad】	in various ways; about various matters [Lit. variously]	いろいろ はなしました。
45.	よく	【Ad】	well [ADVERBIAL FORM OF ii]	よく わかりません。
46.	TIME まえ(に)	【Suf】	...ago	四年(よねん)まえに イギリスへ いきました。

Expressions:

a. ありました。   "Here (OR There) it is!" "I found it!"
b. ああ、そうそう。 "Oh, yes (now I remember)."

Translation of the Examples:

1. The vacation is from December 19th.
2. The vacation is until January 7th.
3. Mr./Ms. Tanaka is a tall person.
4. Korean (language) is different from Japanese.
5. I'm sorry I'm late. [Lit. I have become late and I'm sorry.]
6. I took German (language) in high school.
7. I'll sit next to Michiko.
8. We learned some kanji last week.
9. I received an interesting thing.
10. I showed my friend my new clothes.
11. Dinner is ready! [Lit. Dinner has been made!]
12. Shall I (OR we) take a picture?
13. Please write me a letter.
14. I listen to music often.
15. I don't eat sweets/snacks that often.
16. I eat my (boxed) lunch around one o'clock.
17. We learn various words.
18. We study grammar, too.
19. I'll go to see an old temple.
20. Let's go into the little tea house.
21. There aren't enough seats.
22. My wallet is missing. [Lit. My wallet isn't there.]
23. Is your grandfather well?
24. I talked with an old lady (OR my grandmother).
25. I'm Yoshio Nakamura.
26. I don't have class today.
27. The money is in a different (OR separate) place.
28. My first class is political science.
29. My next class is economics.
30. My last class is history.
36. All the students came.
37. I went home late last night.
38. The classroom is light.
39. This room is dark, isn't it?
40. The dormitory is sometimes noisy.
41. This steak tastes terrible, doesn't it?
42. That's for sure.
43. That's very early (OR fast), isn't it.
44. We talked about various matters.
45. I don't understand well. OR I'm not sure.
46. I went to Great Britain four years ago.

Lesson 10: Grammar

I. The Adverbial Form of i-Type Adjectives and the Copula

Adjectives and the copula (desu) must be changed to their adverbial forms in order to modify verbs (cf. "beautiful" → "beautifully" in English): ADJ-i → -ku; NOUN and na-ADJ (STEM) da → ni.

Although it does not appear in English, naru "become" takes the adverbial form in Japanese.

1. a. こどもは おおきく なりました。 "My child has grown (Lit. became) big."
   b. こどもは げんきに なりました。 "My child has gotten well."
   c. こどもは だいがくせいに なりました。 "My son (OR daughter) has become a college student."

2. けさ はやく おきました。 "I got up early this morning."

3. ひらがなで きれいに かいて ください。 "Please write in hiragana neatly."

4. はじめに きっさてんに はいりました。 "First, we went into a coffee shop."
   つぎに えいがを みました。 "Second (Next), we saw a movie."
   さいごに ホテルで ごはんを たべました。 "Last, we ate in a hotel."

Words such as hajime, tsugi and saigo are nouns and, therefore, take no to modify another noun and ni to modify a verb.

II. The Plain Form in the Present and Past Tenses

In all cases, the past tense is expressed by -ta (and -da with certain verbs), which appears finally. The plain past negative form is formed by changing the present negative form, -nai (which is an i-type adjective), into past, -nakatta.

We will continue to use the plain form in the same contexts as in the last lesson: preceding to omoimasu, to itte imashita, and -deshoo, as well as in noun modification.

(A) I-Type Adjectives

	Pres. Aff.	Pres. Neg.	Past Aff.	Past Neg.
Polite	やすいです	やすく ありません	やすかったです	やすく ありませんでした
Plain	やすい	やすく ない	やすかった	やすく なかった
Polite	いいです	よく ありません	よかったです	よく ありませんでした
Plain	いい	よく ない	よかった	よく なかった

(B) The Copula

	Pres. Aff.	Pres. Neg.	Past Aff.	Past Neg.
Polite	ひまです	ひまじゃ ありません	ひまでした	ひまじゃ ありませんでした
Plain	ひまだ	ひまじゃ ない	ひまだった	ひまじゃ なかった
Polite	よじです	よじじゃ ありません	よじでした	よじじゃ ありませんでした
Plain	よじだ	よじじゃ ない	よじだった	よじじゃ なかった

(C) Verbs

The plain affirmative form in the past tense is formed exactly the same way as the -te form: just change -te into -ta, and -de into -da. (cf. L.7, I.) The past negative form of all verbs end with -nakatta.

u-Verbs:

	Pres. Aff.	Pres. Neg.	Past Aff.	Past Neg.	Other examples
-す	はなす	はなさない	はなした	はなさなかった	
-く	かく	かかない	かいた	かかなかった	きく
EXCEPT:	いく	いかない	いった	いかなかった	------------
-ぐ	いそぐ	いそがない	いそいだ	いそがなかった	
-う	つかう	つかわない	つかった	つかわなかった	あう、いう、おもう...
-つ	たつ	たたない	たった	たたなかった	まつ、もつ
-る	おわる	おわらない	おわった	おわらなかった	ふる、かえる、はいる..
EXCEPT:	ある	ない	あった	なかった	------------
-む	のむ	のまない	のんだ	のまなかった	よむ、つつむ
-ぶ	よぶ	よばない	よんだ	よばなかった	あそぶ
-ぬ	しぬ	しなない	しんだ	しななかった	------------

ru-Verbs:

-iru	たりる	たりない	たりた	たりなかった	いる、みる、できる...
-eru	おしえる	おしえない	おしえた	おしえなかった	あげる、こたえる...

Irregular Verbs:

くる	こない	きた	こなかった
する	しない	した	しなかった

(D) Examples of Plain Form Usage

1. Q: せんしゅう いそがしかったでしょうか。   "I wonder if he was busy last week."
   A: あまり いそがしく なかったでしょう。   "He probably wasn't so busy."

2. Q: しごとは たいへんだったでしょうか。 "I wonder if the job was tough."
　　A: たいへんじゃ なかったと いって いました。 "He said it wasn't tough."

3. この かばんは 三千円(さんぜんえん)だったと おもいます。 "I think this bag was 3,000 yen."
　　　　　　　　　　　PAST [BUT I'M NOT SURE.]

cf. この かばんは 三千円だと おもいました。 "I thought this bag was 3,000 yen."
　　　　　　　　　PRESENT Lit. "I thought, 'This bag is 3,000 yen.'" [BUT I WAS WRONG.]

4. Q: パーティーは おもしろかったと いって いましたか。 "Did he say the party was fun?"
　　A: いいえ、おもしろく なかったと いって いましたよ。 "No, he said it wasn't fun."

5. Q: やましたさんは きのう がっこうへ きたでしょうか。 "Do you suppose Ms. Yamashita came to school yesterday?"
　　A: いいえ、こなかったと おもいます。 "No, I don't think she came."
　　　　　　　PAST　　　　　　PRESENT

cf. こないと おもいました。 "I didn't think she would come."
　　PRESENT　　PAST

6. Q: かわかみさんは みちこさんに あったと おもいますか。 "Do you think Mr. Kawakami saw Michiko?"
　　A: いいえ、あわなかったでしょう。 "No, he probably didn't see her."

III. Noun Modification　cf. L.9, V.

So far we have only used the -te iru form of verbs in noun-modifying (or "relative") clauses. In this lesson we will use various forms of verbs. Remember that the clause comes before the noun that it modifies.

The word order in the clause is the same as that in a simple sentence, i.e., the verb comes at the end; but it must be in the plain form. There are no words in Japanese that correspond to English "relative pronouns," such as who, which and where.

The usage of particles is also the same as that in a simple sentence with the sole exception of wa, which cannot appear in a noun-modifying clause. Use ga (or no) if there is a subject that must be specified, such as when it is different from the subject of the main clause.

The composite of a modifying clause and a noun may appear in sentences of any structure, and it will function as a noun. In other words, the whole phrase may be a subject, direct object, indirect object, location, means, etc.

1. a. ［よく ほんを よむ］ひとは ミラーさんです。
   b. ［あまり ほんを よまない］ひとは ミラーさんです。
   c. ［きのう ほんを よんだ］ひとは ミラーさんです。
   d. ［きのう ほんを よまなかった］ひとは ミラーさんです。

   e. ［いま ほんを よんで いる］ひとは ミラーさんです。
   f. ［いま ほんを よんで いない］ひとは ミラーさんです。
   g. ［さっき ほんを よんで いた］ひとは ミラーさんです。
   h. ［さっき ほんを よんで いなかった］ひとは ミラーさんです。

   a. The person [who reads books often] is Mr. Miller.
   b. The person [who doesn't read much] is Mr. Miller.
   c. The person [who read a book yesterday] was (is) Mr. Miller.
   d. The person [who didn't read a book yesterday] was (is) Mr. Miller.

   e. The person [who is reading a book now] is Mr. Miller.
   f. The person [who isn't reading a book now] is Mr. Miller.
   g. The person [who was reading a book a while ago] was (is) Mr. Miller.
   h. The person [who wasn't reading a book a while ago] was (is) Mr. Miller.

2. a. これは［こどもが (OR の) みる］えいがです。
   b. ここは［がくせいが テープを きく］へやです。
   c. ［（わたしが）あさ よむ］しんぶんは『まいにち しんぶん』です。
   d. ［ビールを のまない］ひとは ジョンソンさんです。

   e. ［せんしゅうの きんようびに いった］パーティーは たいへん にぎやかでした。
   f. ［きのう たべた］やさいは あまり おいしく ありませんでした。
   g. ［こうこうの とき やらなかった］スポーツは やきゅうと すいえいです。
   h. ［きょねん ぎんこうに つとめて いた］ひとは だれですか。

   a. This is a movie [which children see].
   b. This (place) is the room [where the students listen to the tapes].
   c. The newspaper [which I read in the morning] is Mainichi Shimbun.
   d. The person [who doesn't drink beer] is Mr. Johnson.

   e. The party [which I went to last Friday] was very lively.
   f. The vegetables [which I ate yesterday] weren't very good.
   g. The sports [which I didn't do in high school] were (are) baseball and swimming.
   h. Who was (is) the person [who was employed at a bank last year]?

3. a. (わたしは)［ みちこさんが よく いく ］ほんやで じしょを かいました。
   b. ［ (わたしが) めがねを かった ］みせは ゆうびんきょくの うしろに あります。
   c. こんばんは ［ なかむら せんせいが かいた ］しょうせつを よみます。
   d. ［ おおきい くるまを もって いる ］ひとは いません。
   e. ［ こうこうで かがくを おしえて いる ］ひとと アパートに すんで います。
   f. あした ［ ロサンゼルスに きて いる ］にほんじんの ともだちに あいに いきます。
   g. ［ けっこん して いない ］ひとを しって いますか。-- いいえ、しりません。

   a. I bought a dictionary at the bookstore [where Michiko often goes].
   b. The store [where I bought the glasses] is behind the post office.
   c. Tonight I'm going to read the novel [which Prof. Nakamura wrote].
   d. There isn't anyone (a person) [who has a big car].
   e. I live in an apartment with a person [who is teaching science at a high school.]
   f. Tomorrow I'm going (there) to see my Japanese friend [who (has come to and) is in Los Angeles].
   g. Do you know someone (a person) [who isn't married]? -- No, I don't.

If you use the particle ni for location, you need the verb iru or aru "to be (in the sense of existence)." A place of action should be marked with de.

4. a. ［ その つくえの うえに ある ］かみを ください。
   cf. ［ その つくえの うえの ］かみを ください。
   b. ［ あそこに ある ］きかいで きっぷを かって ください。
   c. もりさんは ［ えきの そばに ある ］きっさてんで おくさんを まって います。
   d. ［ まつもとさんの となりに いる ］ひとは よしださんです。
   cf. ［ まつもとさんの となりの ］ひとは よしださんです。
   e. ［ エレベーターの まえに いる ］ひとに きいて ください。
   f. すずきさんは ［ さっき ここに いた ］ひとです。
   cf. すずきさんは ［ さっき ここで でんわを かけて いた ］ひとです。

   a. Please give me the piece of paper [which is on that desk].
   cf. Please give me the piece of paper [on that desk].
   b. Please buy the ticket from (Lit. by) the machine [which is over there].
   c. Mr. Mori is waiting for his wife at the coffee shop [which is near the station].
   d. The person [who is next to Mr. Matsumoto] is Mr. Yoshida.
   cf. The person [next to Mr. Matsumoto] is Mr. Yoshida.
   e. Please ask the person [who is in front of the elevator].
   f. Mr. Suzuki is the person [who was here a while ago].
   cf. Mr. Suzuki is the person [who was making a phone call here a while ago].

だい十一かの あたらしい ことば

1. XやY(やZ) 【P】 X, Y, (Z,) and so forth [JOINS NOUNS] しんぶんや ざっしを よみます。
2. XもYも(Zも) 【P】 both X and Y; neither X nor Y; all (none of) X, Y and Z [INCLUSIVENESS, EMPHATIC] もりさんも おくさんも きます。
3. Xより 【P】 than X きょうとより おおきいです。
4. (Xが) かわく 【u-V】 to get dry くつしたが かわきました。
   かわいて いる [STATE] to be dry くつしたは かわいて います。
5. (Xが) すく 【u-V】 to get empty/uncrowded ちかてつが すきました。
   すいて いる [STATE] to be empty ちかてつは すいて います。
6. (Xが) こむ 【u-V】 to get crowded [Opp. suku] バスが こみました。
   こんで いる [STATE] to be crowded バスは こんで います。
7. (Xを) さがす 【u-V】 to look for; search for X さいふを さがしました。
*8. (Xを) つくる 【u-V】 to make; create X (called) ふくを つくりました。
9. (Xを) やめる 【ru-V】 to quit; give up; not do しごとを やめました。
10. (Xを) はじめる 【ru-V】 to begin; start X はなしを はじめました。 transitive
Rev. (Xが) はじまる 【u-V】 (for X) to begin; start はなしが はじまりました。
11. かまう 【u-V】 to mind わたしは かまいません。
    [ALWAYS USED IN THE NEGATIVE] cf. おかまいなく。(L.7)
12. MODIFIER + ほう 【N】 [EMPHASIZES ONE WHEN COMPARING TWO THINGS, PEOPLE, ETC.]
    とうきょうの ほうが おおきいです。
13. のど 【N】 throat のどが かわきました。
14. おなか 【N】 stomach おなかが すきました。
15. でんしゃ 【N】 train でんしゃで いきましょう。
16. かず 【N】 number へやの かずは しりません。
17. ひ 【N】 day; the sun やすみの ひは おそく おきます。
*18. びじゅつ 【N】 the fine arts せんもんは びじゅつです。
*19. まち 【N】 town; city きょうとは きれいな まちです。
*20. バー 【N】 bar (where one drinks) この バーは くらいですね。
*21. ひがし 【N】 east ワシントンは アメリカの ひがしに あります。
*22. にし 【N】 west ロサンゼルスは アメリカの にしに あります。
*23. みなみ 【N】 south テキサスは アメリカの みなみに あります。
*24. きた 【N】 north ニューヨークは ワシントンの きたに あります。

25.	こっち	【N】	COLLOQUIAL FORM OF こちら	
26.	そっち	【N】	COLLOQUIAL FORM OF そちら	
27.	あっち	【N】	COLLOQUIAL FORM OF あちら	
28.	どっち	【N】	COLLOQUIAL FORM OF どちら	
			which one (of the two) [QW] どっちの ほうが いいですか。	
29.	だいぶつ	【N】	The Big Statue of Buddha	
30.	よしむら	【N】	Yoshimura [SURNAME]	
31.	なら	【N】	Nara [PLACE NAME]	
32.	かまくら	【N】	Kamakura [PLACE NAME]	
*33.	テキサス	【N】	Texas	
34.	むずかしい	【i-A】	difficult	ロシアごは むずかしいです。
*35.	やさしい	【i-A】	easy [Opp. muzukashii]	えいごは やさしいです。
36.	ながい	【i-A】	long	あしたの テストは ながいです。
*37.	みじかい	【i-A】	short [Opp. nagai]	みじかい えんぴつが あります。
38.	あつい	【i-A】	hot	きょうは あついですね。
				あつい コーヒーを のみました。
39.	さむい	【i-A】	cold [Opp. atsui]	きょうは さむいですね。
			[WEATHER, AIR TEMPERATURE ONLY]	
40.	べんり(な)	【na-A】	handy; convenient	この きかいは べんりですよ。
41.	(Xが) すき(な)	【na-A】	fond of X; to like X	わたしは おんがくが すきです。
*42.	(Xと) おなじ	【na-A】	same (as X) [Opp. chigau]	おなじ えいがを にど みました。
			[DOES NOT TAKE na TO MODIFY A NOUN]	
43.	もっと	【Ad】	more; even more...	もっと いい ものを かいます。
44.	ずっと	【Ad】	much more...; far ...er	この ほうが ずっと やすいです。
45.	だいぶ	【Ad】	quite; rather; pretty...	だいぶ あかるく なりました。
46.	これから	【Ad】	from now on; from here	これから どこへ いきますか。
47.	まっすぐ	【Ad】	directly; straight	まっすぐ うちへ かえります。
48.	NOUN かん	【Suf】	[BIG BUILDINGS]	としょかん、えいがかん、びじゅつかん
49.	ADJ (STEM) さ	【Suf】	...ness [CHANGES ADJECTIVES INTO NOUNS]	
			たかさ "height," おおきさ "size," しずかさ "quietness"	

Numbers and Counters:

(A) ～り/にん： ...people

1: ひとり　2: ふたり　3: さんにん　4: よにん　5: ごにん　6: ろくにん
7: しちにん/ななにん　8: はちにん　9: くにん/きゅうにん　10: じゅうにん
11: じゅういちにん　12: じゅうににん　13: じゅうさんにん... なんにん "how many"

(B) ～ばい： ...times (the size, height, etc.); ...fold

1: いちばい　2: にばい　3: さんばい... なんばい "how many times (as big, etc.)"

Translation of the Examples:

1. I read newspapers, magazines, and so forth.
2. Both Mr. Mori and his wife are coming.
3. It's bigger than Kyoto.
4. The socks dried.
   The socks are dry.
5. The subway got less crowded.
   The subway is not crowded.
6. The bus got crowded.
   The bus is crowded.
7. I looked for my wallet.
8. I made a dress.
9. I quit my job.
10. I started my speech (OR talking).
Rev. His speech (OR talk) started.
11. I don't mind. (OR It's o.k. with me.)
    Please don't go to the trouble.
12. Tokyo is bigger.
13. I am (OR became) thirsty.
14. I am (OR became) hungry.
15. Let's go by train.
16. I don't know the number of rooms.
17. I get up late on my days off.
18. My major is art.
19. Kyoto is a pretty city.
20. This bar is dark, isn't it.
21. Washington is in the eastern United States.
22. Los Angeles is in the western United States.
23. Texas is in the southern United States.
24. New York is north of Washington.
28. Which is better?
34. Russian (language) is difficult.
35. English is easy.
36. Tomorrow's test is long.
37. I have a short pencil.
38. It's hot today, isn't it.
    I had hot coffee.
39. It's cold today, isn't it.
40. This machine is convenient.
41. I like music.
42. I saw the same movie twice.
43. I'll buy something better (Lit. a better thing).
44. This is much cheaper.
45. It got quite light.
46. Where are you going now (OR from here)?
47. I'm going straight home.
48. library, movie theater, museum (or fine arts)

だい十一かの ぶんぽう

I. Aは Bが C   [Literally: "As for A, B is/does C."]

In this construction 'A' is the topic (what you are talking about), and the rest of the sentence is the description of that topic. 'B' is the subject of 'C' in the description phrase, "B ga C." The particle <u>wa</u> can be replaced by <u>mo</u> to indicate similarity, and <u>ga</u> can be replaced by <u>mo</u> or <u>wa</u> (for contrast).

1. かわかみさん<u>は</u> せい<u>が</u> たかいです。   "Mr. Kawakami is tall." Lit. "As for Mr. Kawakami, his height is high."

The word meaning "to like" is <u>suki</u>(na), an adjective in Japanese. Therefore, it cannot take the particle <u>o</u>, but takes <u>ga</u>. Do not confuse this word with the verb <u>suku/sukimasu</u> "to get less crowded," which forms an idiomatic expression "to get hungry" with <u>o-naka</u> "stomach" as its subject. <u>Nodo ga kawaku</u> means "to get thirsty." Note that in these phrases the past tense form, <u>-mashita</u>, is used in the affirmative, and the present tense form, <u>-masen</u>, in the negative.

2. わたし<u>は</u> にく<u>が</u> すきです。   "I like meat.
   （わたし<u>は</u>）やさい<u>も</u> すきです。   I like vegetables, too."

cf. しゅじん<u>も</u> にくが すきです。   "My husband likes meat, too."

3. よしお: みちこさん<u>は</u> のど<u>が</u> かわきましたか。   "Are you thirsty, Michiko?"
   みちこ: いいえ、のど<u>は</u> かわきませんが、おなか<u>が</u> すきました。 CONTRAST   "No, I'm not thirsty, but I'm hungry."

II. Comparison Construction

(A) ～ほう

The noun <u>hoo</u> itself does not have any concrete meaning and cannot stand without a modifier. ...Hoo <u>ga</u> + ADJ/ADV means something like "...er; more..." For example, X <u>no</u> <u>hoo</u> <u>ga</u> <u>ii</u> means, "X is better" or "it is better if it is X."

1. A: パーティーは にちようび の ほうが いいですか。   "Is it better if the party is on Sunday?" Lit. "As for the party, is Sunday better?"

   B: いいえ、にちようび じゃ ない ほうが いいです。   "No, it's better if it's not on Sunday."

2. アパートは しずか な ほうが いいです。   "As for an apartment, it's better if it's quiet."

3. A: おちゃは あつ [い] ほうが いいですか。　　　　"Should the tea be hot?"

   B: いいえ、あまり あつ [く ない] ほうが すきです。"No, I like it better if it is not too hot."

(B) Xと Yと どちら (OR どっち) の ほうが...　"Which is more...?"

To answer a question, "<u>dochira</u> (or its colloquial counterpart, <u>dotchi</u>) <u>no hoo ga</u>...," simply replace the question word with the information sought. Make sure to keep the particle <u>ga</u> in your answer because you want to focus on the preceding noun.

4. Q: とうきょうと きょうとと [どちら] の ほうが　"Which is bigger, Tokyo or
      おおきいですか。　　　　　　　　　　　　　　　Kyoto?"

   A: [とうきょう] の ほうが (きょうとより)　　　"TOKYO is bigger (than Kyoto)."
      おおきいです。

Example 5 below is inappropriate as an answer to the question in 4 although it can be used in other situations such as when you are describing Tokyo; the focus in this case is the rest of the sentence.

5. とうきょうは きょうとより おおきいです。　　"Tokyo is BIGGER (than Kyoto)."

6. Q: いぬと ねこと どちらの ほうが すきですか。"Which do you like better, dogs or cats?"

   A1: いぬも ねこも (OR どちらも) すきです。　"I like both (dogs and cats)."

   A2: いぬも ねこも (OR どちらも) すきじゃ　"I don't like either (dogs or
       ありません。　　　　　　　　　　　　　　　cats)."

7. Q: ぶんがくと かがくと どちらの ほうが　　　"Which do you think is more inter-
      おもしろいと おもいますか。　　　　　　　　esting, literature or science?"

   A: ぶんがくの ほうが ずっと おもしろいと　　"I think literature is <u>much</u> more
      おもいます。　　　　　　　　　　　　　　　interesting."

8. Q: たなかさんと さとうさんと どちらの ほうが　"Which person studies harder, Mr.
      よく べんきょう しますか。　　　　　　　　Tanaka or Mr. Sato?"

   A: よく わかりませんが、さとうさんの ほうが　"I'm not sure, but Mr. Sato
      べんきょう するでしょうね。　　　　　　　　probably studies harder."

(C) もっと ...　　"more...; even more..."

Use <u>motto</u> instead of <u>hoo</u> when what is being compared is something you are experiencing at the time, not when you are answering "which" questions. Use it also when you want to say "even more."

9. もっと | あかるい | きっさてんに はいりましょう。
         | しずかな |
         | すいて いる |

"Let's go into a | lighter | coffee shop."
                 | quieter |
                 | less crowded | (=more uncrowded)

10. A: バスは はやいですね。　　　　　　　　"Buses are fast, aren't they?"
    B: ええ、でも、ちかてつは <u>もっと</u> はやいですよ。　"Yes, but subways are <u>even</u> fast<u>er</u>."

III. VERB-た/VERB-ない ほうが いいです   "It's better to do/not to do..."
"You had better (not) do..." "You should (not) do..."

Note that the PAST tense is used when giving affirmative advice, and that the PRESENT negative form is used when giving negative advice.

1. Affirmative: <u>いった</u> ほうが いいですよ。　"You should go."
   Negative: <u>いかない</u> ほうが いいですよ。　"You should not go."

2. Q: まいにち テープを <u>きいた</u> ほうが いいですか。
   "Should I listen to the tape every day?"
   A: ええ、<u>きいた</u> ほうが いいですよ。
   "Yes, you should."

3. Q: ミラーさんも <u>よんだ</u> ほうが いいと おもいますか。
   "Do you think we should invite Mr. Miller, too?"
   A: いいえ、<u>よばない</u> ほうが いいと おもいます。
   "No, I think it's better not to invite him."

4. Q: あまり おそく <u>ならない</u> ほうが いい でしょうね。
   "It would be better for you not to be too late (getting home), right?"
   A: ええ、その ほうが いいです。
   "Yes, that's right (Lit. that'll be better)."

IV. The Plain Form + だろうと おもいます   "I think that probably..."
cf. L.9, IV.

<u>Daroo</u> is the plain form of <u>deshoo</u> "probably." (Remember that the element preceding <u>to</u> omou/omoimasu must be in the plain form.) The addition of <u>daroo</u> makes a sentence sound less certain than without it. Also, use <u>daroo to omoimasu</u> with respect to your own actions when you are uncertain, instead of ending a sentence with ...<u>deshoo</u>. (cf. L.7, III.)

1. やまもとさんは てがみを | かく | だろうと おもいます。
                          | かいた |

"I think Mr. Yamamoto | will probably write | a letter."
                      | probably wrote |

2. Q: こんどの やすみに どこかへ でかけますか。 "Are you going out anywhere this (coming) holiday?"

A: いいえ、どこへも いかない<u>だろう</u>と おもいます。 "No, I probably won't go anywhere (I think)."

3. Q: ジョンソンさんは こんげつ ひまでしょうか。 "I wonder if Mr. Johnson is free this month."

A: いいえ、ひまじゃ ない<u>だろう</u>と おもいます。 "No, he probably isn't, I think."

V. The Plain Form + から and ので

<u>Kara</u> and <u>no de</u> are interchangeable in most cases. However, <u>no de</u> should be used in statements of cause and effect. The reasoning in the case of <u>kara</u> is more subjective; it can be used in any kind of sentence.

It is very common to use the plain form in front of <u>kara</u> and <u>no de</u>, while keeping the main clause in the polite form. The -<u>desu</u>/-<u>masu</u> form is used in a reason clause in very polite situations, especially when one is making requests or extending invitations, and when the clause order is reversed.

1. きのうは いい てんきだった <u>から</u> (OR <u>ので</u>)、 "The weather was good yesterday,
   こうえんへ あそびに いきました。 so we went to the park to play."

2. Reading Comprehension (L.10, p.116):
   …おんがくが うるさい<u>ので</u> すぐ でました。 "We left immediately because the
   　　　　(OR から) music was (Lit. is) loud."

3. いまは ちょっと ようが ある<u>から</u> (OR <u>ので</u>)、 "There's something I have to do
   また あとで きます。 now, so I'll come again later."

4. おなかが すいた<u>から</u>、なにか たべましょうか。 "I'm hungry, so shall we eat
   　　(NOT ので) something?"

Inverted Sentences:

5. ちょっと しつれい します。きゃくが まって います<u>ので</u>。(L.8)

6. じゃ、でんわを して ください。ここに でんわばんごうが あります<u>から</u>。(L.8)

VI. Numbers and Counters　cf. p.77

1. Q: クラスに がくせいは <u>なんにん</u> いますか。 "How many students are there in your class?"

   A: <u>にじゅうよにん</u> います。 "There are twenty-four."

2. ゆうべ <u>ひとり</u>で えいがを みに いきました。 "I went to see a movie by myself (Lit. one person) last night."

3. だいがくの そばに ある アパートに "I live in an apartment, which is near
   ともだちと <u>さんにん</u>で すんで います。 the university, with my two friends." (three of us live together)

だい十二かの あたらしい ことば

1.	NOUN で (たりる)	【P】	with... (it's enough)	千円で たります。(せんえん)
2.	NOUN が	【P】	[OBJECT OF POTENTIAL VERBS]	
3.	(Xが) できる	【ru-V】	can do; can play [POTENTIAL FORM OF suru]	すいえいが できます。
4.	(Xを) たずねる	【ru-V】	to visit; call on X	ともだちを たずねました。
5.	(Xを) ひく	【u-V】	to pull X; catch (cold)	とを ひきました。
6.	つかれる	【ru-V】	to get tired	たいへん つかれました。
	つかれて いる	[STATE]	to be tired	こどもは つかれて います。
7.	こまる	【u-V】	to be at a loss; have trouble	こまりましたねえ。
8.	(Xを) すう	【u-V】	to inhale; smoke X	タバコを すいません。
*9.	(Xを) かむ	【u-V】	to bite; chew X	ガムを かんで います。
10.	VERB-て くる	【kuru】	[ACTION DIRECTED TOWARD THE SPEAKER]	ともだちが たずねて 来ました。(き)
11.	よしゅう	【VN】	preparation (for class)	まい日 よしゅうを します。(にち)
*12.	ふくしゅう	【VN】	review (class material)	ふくしゅうを して 下さい。(くだ)
13.	けいけん	【VN】	experience	けいけんが あります。
14.	アルバイト	【VN】	side/part-time job; summer job	アルバイトを して います。
15.	テニス	【VN】	tennis	わたしは テニスが すきです。
16.	あたま	【N】	head	もりさんは あたまが いいです。
*17.	かみ(の け)	【N】	hair (of the head)	もりさんは かみが ながいです。
*18.	め	【N】	eye(s)	もりさんは めが きれいです。
*19.	はな	【N】	nose	もりさんは はなが たかいです。
*20.	みみ	【N】	ear(s)	みみが いたいです。
*21.	くち	【N】	mouth [PRONOUNCED guchi IN A COMPOUND: yamaguchi]	
22.	は	【N】	tooth; teeth	もりさんは はが 白いです。(しろ)
23.	かぜ	【N】	cold	かぜを ひきました。
*24.	ねつ	【N】	fever	ちょっと ねつが あります。
25.	くに	【N】	country (nation); hometown	アメリカは 大きい くにです。(おお)
26.	りょうしん	【N】	(both) parents	りょうしんは シカゴに います。
27.	ぶっか	【N】	commodity prices	このごろ ぶっかが たかいです。
28.	しょうがっきん	【N】	scholarship (money)	しょうがっきんでは たりません。

29.	そら	【N】	sky	きょうは そらが あおいですね。
30.	タバコ	【N】	tobacco; cigarettes	タバコを かいに いきました。
*31.	ガム	【N】	(chewing) gum	ガムを もって いますか。
*32.	アイスクリーム	【N】	ice cream	アイスクリームを たべましょう。
Rev.	やすみ	【N】	holiday; <u>closed</u> (store, etc.) [ADDITIONAL MEANING]	さかなやは やすみです。
33.	かれ	【N】	he [SOMETIMES, boyfriend]	かれは きょう きません。
34.	かのじょ	【N】	she [SOMETIMES, girlfriend]	ぼくの かのじょです。

<u>Kare</u> AND <u>kanojo</u> CAN BE USED REFERRING TO YOUR CLOSE FRIENDS, BUT NOT TO YOUR SUPERIORS, YOUR OWN FAMILY MEMBERS, OR CHILDREN.

35.	いたい	【i-A】	painful; hurt	おなかが いたいです。
36.	(Xから) とおい	【i-A】	far (from X)	うちは えきから とおいです。
*37.	(Xに) ちかい	【i-A】	close (to X) [Opp. <u>tooi</u>]	うちは えきに ちかいです。
38.	(Xが) じょうず(な)	【na-A】	skillful; good at X	もりさんは えいごが じょうずです。
*39.	(Xが) へた(な)	【na-A】	poor at; bad at X [Opp. <u>joozu</u>]	ぼくは やきゅうが へたです。
40.	きゅうに	【Ad】	suddenly [NOUN + <u>ni</u>]	きゅうに くるまが きました。
41.	ほんとうに	【Ad】	really; truly [NOUN + <u>ni</u>]	ほんとうに たいへんです。 ほんとうですか。
Rev.	たいてい	【N,Ad】	usually; <u>in most cases</u> [ADDITIONAL MEANING]	日本人は たいてい せいが ひくいです。
42.	それでは	【Conj】	well then; in that case (= では、それじゃ、じゃ) [<u>Ja</u> IS A CONTRACTED FORM OF <u>de wa</u>]	
43.	あの(う)	【Int】	Um...; Er...; Well... [SHOWS HESITATION]	
44.	えっ	【Int】	Pardon? What?	

Expressions:

a.	どう したんですか。	"What happened?" "What's the matter?" "What's up?"
b.	じつは ...ん (OR の)です。	"The fact is...; Actually..."
c.	しかたが ありません。	"There's nothing one can do about it." "It can't be helped."
d.	おかげさまで。	"Thanks to you (OR WHOEVER IS RESPONSIBLE)."

Translation of the Examples:

1. 1,000 yen is enough.
3. I can swim. [Lit. I can do swimming.]
4. I visited my friend.
5. I pulled the door.
6. I am (OR got) very tired.
   My child is tired.
7. I'm at a loss. (OR I don't know what to do.)
8. I don't smoke (cigarettes).
9. He/She is chewing gum.
10. My friend came to visit me.
11. I prepare for class every day.
12. Please review (the material).
13. I have experience.
14. I'm working part-time. (OR I have a side job.)
15. I like tennis.
16. Mr./Ms. Mori is smart.
17. Mr./Ms. Mori has long hair.
18. Mr./Ms. Mori has pretty eyes.
19. Mr./Ms. Mori has a nice (Lit. tall) nose.
20. My ear hurts.
22. Mr./Ms. Mori has white teeth.
23. I caught a cold.
24. I have a slight fever.
25. America is a big country.
26. My parents are in Chicago.
27. Prices are high nowadays.
28. A scholarship is not enough.
29. The sky is blue today, isn't it.
30. I went to buy cigarettes.
31. Do you have a piece of gum?
32. Let's eat ice cream.
Rev. The fish store is closed.
33. He's not coming today.
34. This is my girlfriend.
35. My stomach hurts. (OR I have a stomachache.)
36. My house is far from the station.
37. My house is close to the station.
38. Mr./Ms. Mori's English is good.
39. I'm terrible at baseball.
40. A car came all of a sudden.
41. It's really tough.
    Really?
Rev. Most Japanese people are short.

だい十二かの ぶんぽう

I. More Examples of 'Aは Bが C'

1. a. 田中さんは おんがくが すきです。　　　　"Mr. Tanaka likes music."
   b. [おんがくが すきな] 人は 田中さんです。"The person [who likes music] is Mr. Tanaka."
2. a. 田中さんは あたまが いいです。　　　　"Mr. Tanaka is smart." Lit. "As for Mr. Tanaka, his head is good."
   b. [あたまが いい] 人は 田中さんです。"The person [who is smart] is Mr. T."
3. a. 田中さんは お金が あります。　　　　"Mr. Tanaka has money."
   b. [お金が ある] 人は 田中さんです。"The person [who has money] is Mr. T."
4. (私は) おなかが いたいです。　　　　"I have a stomachache." Lit. "As for myself, my stomach hurts."

II. VERB-て 下さいませんか　"Won't/Will you please do...?"　[POLITE REQUEST]

Addition of -masen ka to ...te kudasai makes the request sound politer.

1. ゆっくり はなして 下さいませんか。　　　"Won't you please speak slowly?"
cf. ゆっくり はなして 下さい。　　　　　　"Please speak slowly."
2. すみませんが、この かみに じゅうしょと　"Excuse me, but will you please write
   おなまえを かいて 下さいませんか。　　 your address and name on this paper?"

III. CLAUSE (PLAIN) ん (OR の)です　"It is that..." ".... That's why." [EXPLANATION]

No desu (OR n desu in speech) is attached to a sentence ending in the plain form. One exception is that instead of da, na appears for NOUN/na-ADJ desu. Be careful not confuse this na with the stem of the negative word nai.

N(o) desu is related to no de indicating reasons. Its basic function is to explain an on-going situation or a situation which has been or will be stated or implied in another sentence. In conversation it sounds emphatic and often elicits a sympathetic or attentive reaction from the listener.

i-ADJ:　おいしいんです、　おいしく ないんです、　おいしかったんです...
na-ADJ:　ひま な んです、　ひまじゃ ないんです、　ひまだったんです...
NOUN:　やすみ な んです、　やすみだったんです、　やすみじゃ なかったんです...
VERB:　いくんです、　いかないんです、　いったんです、　いかなかったんです...

(A) In statements: ...んです。   "It's that..."   ".... That's why."

1. a. 今日は パーティーへ 行きません。 "I'm not going to the party today. I
      いそがしい<u>ん</u>です。[EXPLANATION]   am busy. That's why. (OR It's that
                                            I'm busy.)"
   b. ....おきゃくさんが 来る<u>ん</u>です。 "The guests are coming. That's why."
   c. ....くるまが ない<u>ん</u>です。   "I don't have a car. That's why."
   d. ....あしたは テスト な<u>ん</u>です。 "Tomorrow is the test. That's why."

2. Phone Conversation between Smith and Michiko's mother:

   S: もしもし、スミスですが、みち子さんを おねがいします。
   M: あ、みち子は いま いない<u>ん</u>ですよ。 "Oh, (it's that) Michiko isn't here now.
      また あとで かけて 下さいませんか。   Won't you please call her again later?"

3. A: あの 人は 日本語が じょうずですね。   "His Japanese is good, isn't it?"
   B1: ええ、でも、子どもの 時 日本に すんで "Yes, but he lived in Japan when
       いた<u>ん</u>です。   he was a child."
   B2: ...おくさんが 日本人 な<u>ん</u>です。 "...his wife is Japanese."
   B3: ...十年前から ならって いる<u>ん</u>です。 "...he's been learning it for ten
                                            years (Lit. from ten years ago)."

["Therefore, he should be good" IS IMPLIED IN ALL THE ABOVE RESPONSES.]

(B) In conjecture: ...んでしょう。   "It's probably that..."
                                      ".... That's probably why."

With ...<u>n deshoo</u> you are guessing a possible explanation for a given situation based on some EVIDENCE you observe.

4. A: ジョンソンさんは いませんね。   "Mr. Johnson isn't here, is he?"
   B1: ええ、うちへ かえった<u>ん</u>でしょう。 "No, he must have gone home.
                                            (That's probably why.)"
   B2: ええ、でんしゃが おそく なった<u>ん</u>でしょう。 "No, the train must have been
                                            late."
   B3: ええ、かぜを ひいた<u>ん</u>でしょう。 "No, he must have caught a cold."
   B4: ええ、まだ ねて いる<u>ん</u>でしょう。 "No, he must still be sleeping."

The following sentence, which lacks <u>n(o)</u>, is appropriate when you are simply guessing what he is doing now, but <u>not</u> to explain his absence.

cf. まだ ねて いるでしょう。   "He is probably still sleeping."

(C) In questions:　...んですか。

　　...N desu ka questions are extremely common in conversation. However, they often carry surprised or accusatory overtones, as well as showing the questioner's concern for or closeness toward the other party at other times, so be careful about when to use it and when not to use it.

Yes/no-questions:　"Is it that...?"　"Am I correct in assuming that...?"
　　　　　　　　　　"Do you mean (to say that)...?"

　　Unlike a regular yes/no-question, ...n desu ka questions do not seek a simple "yes" or "no" answer. Rather, it asks for a confirmation of what one observes (based on some evidence) and/or an explanation for it.

5.　どこかへ でかけるんですか。　　"You mean you're going out somewhere?"　OR
　　　　　　　　　　　　　　　　　　"Is it that you are going out somewhere?"
　　　　　　　　　　　　　　　　　　(Is that why you are so dressed up?　etc.)

cf.　どこかへ でかけますか。　　　"Are you going out somewhere?" [NO ASSUMPTION]

6.　SEEING SOMEONE WITH A WET UMBRELLA:
　　あめが ふって いるんですか。　"Is it that it's raining?"
　　　　　　　　　　　　　　　　　　[ASKS FOR A CONFIRMATION]

7.　SEEING THAT SOMEONE WHO IS SUPPOSED TO HAVE LEFT IS STILL IN HIS ROOM:
　　A: まだ いるんですか。　　　　"Are you still here?" [ASKS FOR AN EXPLANATION]
　　B: ええ、さいふが ないんです。　"Yes, I can't find my wallet. (That's why.)"

Wh-questions:

8.　何を して いるんですか。　　"What on earth are you doing?"　OR
　　　　　　　　　　　　　　　　　"What are you doing? (I really want to know!)"

cf.　何を して いますか。　　　　"What are you doing?" [NO PARTICULAR OVERTONE]

9.　A: どう したんですか。　　　　"What's the matter?"
　　B: あたまが いたいんです。　　"(It's that) I have a headache."

(D) More examples:

10.　SEEING THAT SOMEONE IS MAKING A FACE WHEN HE EATS:　まずいんですか。
11.　もう 一ど 言って 下さいませんか。よく 分からなかったんです。
12.　A: 山下さんは かおが あかいですね。　B: ええ、ビールを のんだんでしょう。
13.　A: どうして 日本語を べんきょう して いるんですか。
　　　B: 日本が すきなんです。（OR　日本が すきだからです。）
14.　A: これから モスクワへ 行きます。　B: えっ？ モスクワへ 行くんですか。

10. Does it taste bad?
11. Won't you please say it again?   (It's that) I didn't understand well.
12. A: Mr. Yamashita's face is red, isn't it?   B: Yes, he must have had some beer.
13. A: Why are you studying Japanese?   B: I like Japan. (That's why.)
14. A: I'm going to Moscow now.   B: What? (Did you say) you're going to Moscow?

IV. VERB₁ (STEM)-ながら VERB₂   "(I) do V₁ while doing V₂."

This pattern expresses that two actions are performed at the same time by the same person(s). The ...<u>nagara</u> part describes how the main action, appearing at the end of the sentence, is carried out. (In English the main action is often indicated in the "while"-clause.) Remember that the stem cannot indicate tenses.

1. (私は) たいてい しんぶんを よみながら あさごはんを たべます。
   <u>MAIN ACTION</u>
   "I usually read the newspaper while eating breakfast."

2. 川上さんは ゆうべ テレビを みながら しごとを しました。
   "Last night Mr. Kawakami watched TV while he worked."

3. A: 山本さんたちは 今 何を して いますか。
   "What is Mr. Yamamoto and others doing now?"

   B: レコードを ききながら はなしを しています。
   "They are talking while listening to records."

4. コーヒーを のみながら まちましょう。
   "Let's have coffee while we wait."

※ それでいながら = even so, even if it's the case

V. CLAUSE (PLAIN) の (= NOUN PHRASE)   "to do...; doing..."

<u>No</u> makes a clause into a noun phrase so that the phrase can be used as a subject, object, etc. Just as one cannot say "I like read" or "Read is fun" but must say "I like <u>to</u> read" or "Read<u>ing</u> is fun" in English, Japanese uses <u>no</u> in such situations.

1. [しょうせつを よむ] <u>の</u>は おもしろいです。
   "It's fun [to read novels]." OR
   "[Reading novels] is fun."

2. [タバコを すう] <u>の</u>は よく ありませんよ。
   "[Smoking (cigarettes)] is not good, you know."

3. A: [テープを きく] <u>の</u>は つまらないと おもいますか。
   "Do you find it boring [to listen to the tape]?"

   B: ええ、ときどき...
   "Yes, sometimes..."

4. [アルバイトを しながら べんきょう する] <u>の</u>は たいへんでしょうね。
   "Working part-time while going to school (Lit. studying) is probably tough, isnt it?"

- 89 -

VI. CLAUSE (PLAIN) かも しれません。 "maybe...; may...; might..."

Ka and mo are particles, and the verb shiremasen/shirenai is always in the negative. (Do not confuse this with the negative form of shiru "to find out," which is shirimasen/shiranai.) This set phrase itself is not inflected: affirmative-negative and present-past distinctions precede it. (Exception: The copula da is deleted in the present tense affirmative.)

1. あの みせは | たかい / たかく ない | かも しれません。 "That store may be expensive." / "That store may not be expensive."

2. この じしょは | べんり / べんりじゃ ない | かも しれません。 "This dictionary may be handy." / "This dictionary may not be handy."

3. しずかな | まち / まちだった | かも しれません。 "It may be a quiet town." / "It may have been a quiet town."

4. ゆきが | ふる / ふらない / ふった / ふらなかった / ふって いる | かも しれません。 "It may snow." / "It may not snow." / "It may have snowed." / "It may not have snowed." / "It may be snowing."

5. Degrees of certainty:
   a. きます。 "He will come."
   b. くる（だろう）と おもいます。 "I think he will (probably) come."
   c. くるでしょう。 "He will probably come."
   d. くるかも しれません。 "He might come."

VII. 〜ました vs. 〜て います (when indicating sensations)

...Mashita is used to express the speaker's own present sensations such as being hungry, thirsty, and tired. ...Te imasu is used to indicate the third person's present sensation or when the speaker states it objectively, e.g., "Come to think of it, I am tired." ...Mashita can also indicate a change of state in the past: "I/he got tired." Use ...te imashita for all persons to indicate a past state: "I/he was tired," etc.

1. a. （私は）のどが かわきました。 "I'm thirsty."
   b. 子どもは のどが かわいて いると おもいます。 "I think my child is thirsty."

2. a. ああ、つかれました。（OR ああ、つかれた。） "Gee, I'm tired."
   b. しゅじんは このごろ つかれて います。 "My husband has been tired lately."
   c. きのうは つかれて いましたが、りょうしん に てがみを かきました。 "Although I was tired, I wrote a letter to my parents yesterday."

だい十三かの あたらしい ことば

1. XかY(かZ) 【P】 either X or Y (or Z) [ALTERNATIVE] しんぶんか ざっしを 読(よ)みます。
2. TIME SPAN で 【P】 (with)in [REQUIRED TIME] えいがは 十分(じっぷん)で はじまります。
3. Xに ついて 【PPhr】 about; concerning X おんがくに ついて 話(はな)しました。
4. (Xを) あつめる 【ru-V】 to collect; gather X お金(かね)を あつめます。
5. (さかなが) つれる 【ru-V】 (for fish) to be caught; be able to catch (fish) さかなが たくさん つれました。
6. (さかなを) つる 【u-V】 to fish; catch (fish) さかなを たくさん つりました。
7. (Xが) なる 【u-V】 (for X) to ring でんわが なって います。
*8. (Xに) つく 【u-V】 to arrive in/at X *(Motion intrans.)* あした シカゴに つきます。
Rev. (Xを) ひく 【u-V】 to pull X; catch (cold) + ADDITIONAL MEANINGS: to play (a musical instrument) *with strings*; to look up (words) ピアノを ひきます。 / じしょで ことばを ひきます。
9. VERB (STEM)-だす 【u-V】 to start/begin doing... [AUXILIARY VERB] あめが ふりだしました。 *usually involuntary actions (raining...)*
10. VERB-て みる 【ru-V】 to do... and see/find out; to try doing... [AUXILIARY VERB] おかしを 食(た)べて みました。
11. つり 【VN】 fishing [STEM OF tsuri-masu] つりに 行(い)きましょう。
12. ようじ (= よう) 【N】 errand; something to attend to
13. よてい 【N】 plan; schedule 今日(きょう)は よていが あります。
14. ろんぶん 【N】 thesis; dissertation [bun MEANS "sentence" -- cf. bun-gaku, bun-poo] ろんぶんを かきます。
15. しりょう 【N】 (source) material; data しりょうを あつめます。
16. きぎょう 【N】 enterprise 大(おお)きい きぎょうです。
17. こよう せいど 【N】 employment system こよう せいどが ちがいます。
*18. だいがくいん 【N】 graduate school 大学(だいがく)いんに 入(はい)ります。
19. にっき 【N】 diary にっきを かいて います。
*20. て 【N】 hand(s); (SOMETIMES, arm) てが いたいんです。
*21. あし 【N】 foot/feet; leg(s) かれは あしが ながいです。
*22. ピアノ 【N】 piano ピアノを ならって います。
*23. ギター 【N】 guitar ギターを ひいて 下(くだ)さい。
24. いとう 【N】 / Ito [SURNAME]

*25.	しゅうまつ	【N】	weekend	週まつに 何を しますか。
26.	さらいしゅう	【N,Ad】	week after next	来週か さ来週 また 来ます。
27.	ことし	【N,Ad】	this year	今年 けっこん します。
28.	らいねん	【N,Ad】	next year	来年の 六月まで 日本に います。
29.	さらいねん	【N,Ad】	year after next	さ来年から しごとを します。
30.	おととし	【N,Ad】	year before last	おととし アルバイトを しました。
31.	CLAUSE-あいだ	【N,Ad】	while (during the period when)...	
				日本に いる あいだに ろんぶんを かきます。
*32.	うれしい	【i-A】	glad; happy	たいへん うれしいです。
*33.	ねむい	【i-A】	sleepy	ちょっと ねむいんです。
34.	だいじょうぶ(な)	【na-A】	all right; no problem	だいじょうぶですか。
35.	ながく	【Ad】	for a long time	おきゃくさんは ながく いました。
			[ADVERBIAL FORM OF nagai]	
*36.	もう すぐ	【Ad】	soon; before long	もう すぐ 休みに なります。
REV.	すぐ	【Ad】	soon; immediately (L.4)	
37.	いっしょに	【Ad】	together; with me	いっしょに 行きましょう。
			[NOUN + ni]	
38.	ところで	【Conj】	by the way	ところで、今 何時ですか。
			[NOUN + de]	
39.	けれども	【Conj】	however; but	川上さんに でんわを かけました。
			[CONTRACTED FORM: kedo]	けれども、いませんでした。
40.	うん	【Int】	yeah [INFORMAL, SOMETIMES RUDE, "yes"]	
41.	～へん	【Suf】	...area	
	この へん	【N】	this area; around here	この へんが 良いですよ。
	その へん	【N】	that area; around there [CLOSE TO THE HEARER]	
	あの へん	【N】	that area; around there [FAR AWAY]	
	どの へん	【N】	which area; whereabouts [QW]	
				おたくは ニューヨークの どのへんですか。
42.	おもったより	【Phr】	more than I had thought/expected [omotta + yori]	
				テストは おもったより むずかしかったです。

Expression:

a. ようじが できました。 "Something came up."

*b. おめでとう ございます。 "Congratulations!" "Happy Birthday (New Year, etc.)."

Translation of the Examples:

1. I'll read either the newspaper or a magazine.
2. The movie will start in ten minutes.
3. We talked about music.
4. I'll collect money.
5. A lot of fish were caught.
6. I caught a lot of fish.
7. The phone is ringing.
8. I'll arrive in Chicago tomorrow.

Rev. I play the piano.
  I look up words in a dictionary.

9. It started raining.
10. I ate the sweets to see (how they would taste).
    (OR I tried the sweets.)
11. Let's go fishing.
13. I have plans today.
14. I'll write my dissertation.
15. I'll collect source material (OR data).
16. It's a big enterprise.
17. The employment system is different.
18. I'll go to (Lit. enter) a graduate school.
19. I'm writing a diary.
20. My hand (OR arm) hurts.
21. He has long legs.
22. I'm taking piano lessons.
23. Please play the guitar.
25. What do you do on weekends?
26. I'll come again either next week or the week after.
27. I'm getting married this year.
28. I'll stay in Japan until June of next year.
29. I'll work starting the year after next.
30. I worked part-time the year before last.
31. I'll write my dissertation while I'm in Japan.
32. I'm very glad.
33. I'm a little sleepy.
34. Are you all right?
35. The guests stayed long.
36. It'll be a vacation soon.
37. Let's go together.
38. By the way, what time is it?
39. I called Mr. Kawakami. However, he wasn't there.
41. This area is good, you know.
    Whereabouts in New York is your home?
42. The test was harder than I had expected.

だい十三かの ぶんぽう

I. ADJ/VERB (STEM)-そう　"It looks as if (it) will/would be..."
　　　　　　　　　　　　　　"It seems that..."　"It sounds..."

Stem + <u>soo</u> expresses a speaker's impression based on the senses, particularly sight, prior to the actual discovery or occurrence of an action or state. When one uses this expression, one is guessing about something and does not know it for a fact.

-<u>Soo</u> is conjugated just like a <u>na</u>-type adjective with respect to what follows it; it takes <u>na</u> to modify a noun and <u>ni</u> to modify a verb. It is very common for the speaker to add the particle <u>ne</u> after ...<u>soo desu</u> and ...<u>soo na</u> NOUN <u>desu</u> in speech to get a response from the listener.

Stems are obtained as follows:　<u>i</u>-ADJ minus <u>i</u>;　<u>na</u>-ADJ minus <u>na</u>; and VERB-<u>masu</u> minus <u>masu</u>. However, the -<u>soo</u> forms of <u>ii</u> and <u>nai</u> are <u>yosa-soo</u> and <u>nasa-soo</u>, respectively.

(A) With i-Adjectives:

1. a. この おかしは <u>おいしそう</u>ですね。　　"This cake looks (as if it would be) delicious, doesn't it?"

   b. <u>おいしそうな</u> おかしですね。　　"It's delicious-looking cake, isn't it?"

   c. 子どもは <u>おいしそうに</u> おかしを 食べて います。　　"The child is eating cake looking as if it were delicious."

   d. おかしは <u>おいしそう</u>だった (OR 〜でした) から、たくさん 買いました。　　"The cake looked delicious, so I bought a lot of it."

2. a. その 本は <u>おもしろそう</u>ですね。 = <u>おもしろそうな</u> 本ですね。

   b. 山本さんは [おもしろそう／つまらなそう] に ともだちと 話して いました。　　"Mr. Yamamoto was talking with his friends, looking as if it were fun/boring."

3. はやしさんは あたまが <u>いたそう</u>です。　　"It seems as though Ms. Hayashi has a headache."

4. a. ここ [が] <u>よさそう</u>ですね。　　"THIS place seems good, doesn't it?"

   cf. ここ [は] <u>よさそう</u>ですね。　　"This place seems GOOD, doesn't it?"

5. a. あの 人は あまり お金が <u>なさそう</u>ですね。(←ない ← NEGATIVE OF ある)
   "He doesn't seem to have much money, does he?"

   b. この みせは たかく <u>なさそう</u>ですよ。(←たかく ない ← NEGATIVE OF たかい)
   "This store doesn't seem expensive."

- 94 -

c. さとうさんは ひまじゃ なさそうです。(←ひまじゃ ない ← NEGATIVE OF ひまだ)
"Mr. Sato doesn't seem to be free."

(B) With na-Adjectives:

6. a. この きかいは べんりそうですね。   "This machine looks handy, doesn't it?"
   b. べんりそうな きかいですね。   "It's a handy-looking machine, isn't it?"
   c. べんりそうだ (OR 〜です) から、   "It looks handy, so shall we try (using)
      つかって みましょうか。   it?"

7. 子どもたちは げんきそうに あそんで   "The children are playing looking as if
   います。   they're full of energy."

8. すずきさんの おくさんは テニスが   "Mrs. Suzuki looks like a good tennis
   じょうずそうですね。   player, doesn't she?"

(C) With Verbs: "It seems/looks like SOMETHING is going to HAPPEN;
                     It seems/looks like SOMEONE will/can do..."

<u>VERB (STEM)-soo is usually used with "non-controllable" verbs -- those</u> which describe something that happens or how things are, rather than what the speaker does under his own volition. They include verbs such as <u>huru</u>, <u>aru</u> and <u>konde iru</u>, as well as all "potential" verbs such as <u>wakaru</u> "(can) understand" and <u>dekiru</u> "can do/play." When it is used with regular ("controllable") verbs, then the speaker is guessing about someone else's actions.

9. a. 雨が ふりそうですね。   BOTH a. AND b. MEAN, "It looks like it's
   b. 雨が ふりそうな てんきですね。   going to rain, doesn't it?"
   c. 雨が ふりそうでした。   "It look<u>ed</u> as if it were going to rain."
   d. 雨は ふりそうじゃ ありません。   "It does <u>not</u> look like it's going to rain."

10. 今日は アルバイトが 早く おわりそうです。(← おわる)
11. 先週は テストが なかったから、今週は ありそうです。(←ある)
12. さかなが たくさん つれそうですね。(←つれる)
13. しゅ人は 今ばんも おそく かえって 来そうです。(←かえって 来る)
14. やくに たちそうな じしょですね。(←やくに たつ)
15. この きっさてんは こんで いそうだから、やめた ほうが いいですね。(←こんで いる)

10. It looks like my (part-time) job will be finished early today.
11. Since there wasn't a test last week, it looks like there'll be one this week.
12. It seems like we can catch many fish, doesn't it?
13. It looks like my husband will come home late again (also) tonight.
14. It's a useful-looking dictionary, isn't it?
15. This coffee shop looks crowded, so we had better <u>not go in</u> (give up), huh?

- 95 -

II. VERB (PRES.) よていです   "(I) plan to do..." "(My) plan is to do..."
                              "(It) is scheduled to..."

Yotee is a noun meaning "plan; schedule." This pattern expresses one's plan, usually having to do with scheduling something, but not trivial matters that take little effort.

1. A: 来年は 何を する よていですか。   "What do you plan to do next year?"
   B: 日本へ 行って、けいざいを べんきょう   "I plan to go to Japan and study
      する よていです。   economics."

2. A: ひこうきは 何時に ワシントンを でますか。 "What time does the plane leave
                                                  Washington?"
   B: 午前 八時 二十分に でる よていです。   "It's scheduled to leave at 8:20
                                                  a.m."

III. The Volitional Form of Verbs

In informal speech the volitional form is used by men as the plain form counterpart of -mashoo, "let's do...," at the end of sentences, while in polite speech it is used by both men and women in certain fixed patterns to indicate one's "intention." This form appears only in the affirmative.

In the case of u-verbs, replace the final syllable with the bottom-row sound in the hiragana syllabary, -o, and pronounce it long. For ru-verbs, drop -ru and add -yoo. (Be sure to write the hiragana symbol for this yo in the normal size, not small.)

u-Verbs: はなす → はなそう、きく → きこう、あう → あおう、まつ → まとう
            とる → とろう、のむ → のもう...
ru-Verbs: おきる → おきよう、みる → みよう、おしえる → おしえよう...
Irregular Verbs: くる → こよう、する → しよう

(A) VERB (VOL.) と おもって います   "(I) am/have been thinking of doing..."
                                        "(I) am/have been planning to do..."

This pattern expresses one's "intention" or "plan." One could be speaking of trivial or serious matters. Compared to ...yotee desu, it sounds more subjective and/or tentative.

1. A: 来年は 何を する よていですか。   "What do you plan to do next year?"
   B: 日本へ 行って、けいざいを べんきょう   "I'm thinking of going to Japan and
      しようと おもって います。   studying economics." (cf. II-1.)

- 96 -

2. a. こんどの 金よう日に えいがを 見に 行こう と おもって います。   "I'm planning to go see a movie this Friday."

   cf. こんどの 金よう日に えいがを 見に 行く (だろう)と おもいます。   "I think I/he will (probably) see a movie this Friday." [BUT I'M NOT SURE]

   b. えいがを 見に 行こうと おもって いました (が、やめました)。   "I was thinking of going to see a movie (but I gave up the idea)."

3. かぜを ひいたから、早く かえろうと おもって います。   "I'm thinking of going home early because I've caught a cold."

(B) VERB (VOL.)と した 時   "When (I) was about to do..., SOMETHING HAPPENED." "Just as (I) was going to do..., ..."

Shita here does not have the usual meaning of "did," but is closer to "thought" in meaning. (In fact, it can be substituted with omotta without changing the basic meaning.) The to preceding it is the quotation particle.

1. けさ でかけようと した 時、雨が ふりだしました。   "When I was about to go out this morning, it started raining."

2. A: きのう かった レコードを ききましたか。   "Did you listen to the records you bought yesterday?"

   B: いいえ、じつは、きこうと した 時、りょうしんが たずねて 来たんです。   "No, the fact is my parents came to visit me when I was about to listen to them."

IV. CLAUSE (X) けれども、CLAUSE (Y)   "X, but Y." "Y although X."

Keredomo (and its contracted form kedo) is a conjunctive particle similar to ga, "but," in meaning. While ga always follows the polite form in polite speech, keredomo is very often attached to the plain form even when the main sentence is in the polite form. Keredomo, like demo, can also be used to start a sentence, which ga cannot.

1. a. 川上さんの うちへ 行きました。けれども、だれも いませんでした。   "I went to Mr. Kawakami's house. However, nobody was home."

   b. 川上さんの うちへ 行ったけれども (OR けど)、だれも いませんでした。   "I went to Mr. Kawakami's house, but nobody was home."

   cf. 川上さんの うちへ 行きましたが、だれも いませんでした。   [SAME AS 1-b.]

2. Dialogue (ll. 20-21, p.144):
   ぼくも 行こうと おもって いたんだけど、ざんねんだった。   "I was thinking of going, too, but it was too bad (that I couldn't go)."

V. The -te Form Indicating Reasons   "(I) am glad (sorry, etc.) that..."
                                     "(It) is..., and so..."
                                        cf. L.6, I. and L.7, I.

   1) The -te form is more appropriate than kara and no de to express the reason (or cause) of certain states, especially emotions and sensations.

   2) The -te form indicating reasons can only be used when the main clause expresses facts, but not requests, advice, proposals, the speaker's intentional actions, etc.

   3) The -te form basically means "and," and it does not indicate reasons as clearly as kara and no de do. As an answer to a "why" question, use kara or no de, not te.

   4) The -te form (of any sort) does not carry tenses; the present-past distinction is indicated at the end of the sentence. However, it often implies that an action (or non-action) in the first clause is completed before the main clause occurs. The interpretation depends on the context, as shown in Examples 1 and 2 below.

   5) There are affirmative and negative forms for every -te form. The negative -te form for indicating reasons is ...naku-te, deriving from ...nai, which is an i-adjective. (See Example 2.)

   6) The subject of a subordinate clause, including reason clauses, is marked by the particle ga if it is different from the main clause subject which is usually marked by wa when expressed. (See Examples 2 and 5.)

1. おそく なって すみません。　　　　　　　"I'm sorry I'm late." Lit. "I have become late and I'm sorry."
2. 山下さん が 来なくて ざんねんですね。　　"It's too bad that Mr. Yamashita didn't come, isn't it?"
3. 今日は 日よう日で、本やは 休みです。　　"Today is Sunday, so the bookstore is closed."
4. ここは うるさくて、べんきょうが できません。"This place is noisy, so I can't study."
   　　　　　　　　(NOT しません)
5. ジョンソンさんは よう が あって、　　　"Ms. Johnson had an errand, and so she didn't come to the party."
   パーティーへ 来ませんでした。

   In the following example, both iku "go" and oshieru "teach" are verbs of intentional actions. Therefore, the -te form simply means "and" and indicates a chronological order, not a reason.

cf. フランスへ 行って、英語を おしえます。"I'm going to France and teach English."
                       おしえました。"I went to France and taught English."

VI. Time Clauses with 'toki' and 'aida'

The tense is usually kept in the present (or in the noun-modifying form) within a time clause that ends with a stative word. The stative words are nouns, adjectives and verbs expressing states, such as <u>iru</u> and <u>aru</u> (rather than actions and events), and negatives. This is true regardless of whether the main clause is in the present or past tense.

1. 子どもの／ひまな／わかい 時、しょうせつを 読みました。 "I read novels when I <u>was</u> a child. / I <u>was</u> free. / I <u>was</u> young."

2. (私は) ぎんこうに つとめて いる (OR いた) 時、みち子さんに あいました。 "I met Michiko when I was working for a bank."

cf. ドイツへ 行った 時、みち子さんに あいました。 "...when I went to Germany."

3. くるま が ない 時は あるいて 学校へ 行きました。 "When I didn't have a car, I walked to school."

...<u>Aida ni</u> "during the period when..." indicates point of time due to the presence of the particle <u>ni</u>, while ...<u>aida wa</u> "for the whole time..." indicates duration of time.

<u>Aida</u> (<u>ni/wa</u>) is quite different from ...<u>nagara</u> "while doing..." (L.12). It expresses <u>when</u> the main verb is carried out, while <u>nagara</u> specifies <u>how</u> it is done. <u>Nagara</u> takes only ACTION verbs on both sides of it, and the subjects of the verbs must be the same person(s). In contrast, <u>aida</u> follows a description of a STATE, such as being in a place or being engaged in actions, and the subjects can be the same or different. Also, while the stem of a verb precedes <u>nagara</u>, a noun-modifying form precedes <u>aida</u>.

4. (私は) 子ども が ねて いる <u>あいだに</u>、べんきょうを します。(NOT ながら) "I'll study while the kids are sleeping."

cf. (私は) コーヒーを のみ<u>ながら</u> べんきょうを します。 "I drink coffee while studying."

5. Dialogue (11.7-8, p.144):
その (= 日本に いる) <u>あいだに</u> ろんぶんの しりょうを あつめようと おもって います。 "I'm thinking of collecting materials for my thesis during that time (while I'm in Japan)."

6. Dialogue (1.18, p.144):
つって いる <u>あいだは</u> (てんきは) だいじょうぶ だったよ。 "(The weather) was good (Lit. o.k.) while we were fishing."

だい十四かの あたらしい ことば

1.	TIME までに	【P】	by...; on or before... [DEADLINE]	五時までに 来て 下さい。
Rev.	TIME まで		until...	五時まで まって 下さい。
2.	PERSON に	【P】	from...to [SOURCE]	友だちに 話を 聞きました。
3.	(Xに Yを) かりる	【ru-V】	to borrow (Y from X)	友だちに 本を かります。
4.	(Xに Yを) かす	【u-V】	to lend (Y to X)	友だちに 本を かします。
5.	(Xを) しらべる	【ru-V】	to check; investigate	しらべて みます。
6.	(Xが) もどる	【u-V】	(for X) to return _somewhere_ _kaeru→home_	てがみが もどりました。
7.	(Xが) やすむ	【u-V】	(for X) to rest [yasumi: STEM OF yasumi-masu]	休んだ 方が いいですよ。
	(Xを) やすむ		to be absent (from X)	今日 学校を 休みました。
8.	(Xを) おこす	【u-V】	to wake X up	子どもを おこしました。
Rev.	(Xが) おきる	【ru-V】	(for X) to wake up	子どもが おきました。
Rev.	(Xを) つかう	【u-V】	to use X; spend (money) [ADDITIONAL MEANING]	お金を たくさん つかいました。
*9.	(Xを) だす	【u-V】	to take X out; to turn in (homework, etc.); to mail (a letter)	ノートを だして 下さい。 しゅくだいを だしました。 てがみを だしました。
10.	VERB (STEM)-だす	【u-V】	① to do... out (of a room, building, etc.); [AUXILIARY VERB] ② to start doing... (L.13)	もちだす、かりだす、... 雨が ふりだしました。 _started to rain_
11.	かしだし	【VN】	lending service (library, lang. lab., etc.) [STEM OF kashi-dashi-masu]	かしだしが できます。
12.	しょくじ	【VN】	dining; meal	ホテルで しょくじを します。
13.	かいぎ	【VN】	meeting; conference	かいぎが はじまります。
14.	タイプ	【VN,N】	typing; typewriter	このタイプを つかいます。
*15.	しゅくだい	【VN】	homework assignment	しゅくだいが あります。
*16.	うんどう	【VN】	(physical) exercise	毎日 うんどうを します。
17.	きかん	【N】	period; term [ki + kan]	きかんは 三日です。
*18.	がっき	【N】	school term [gak + ki]	先学き、今学き、来学き
*19.	(お)しょうがつ	【N】	New Year's Day	おしょう月は どうでしたか。

20.	いしゃ	【N】	(medical) doctor [cf. i-gaku "medical science"]	いしゃに なるかも しれません。
21.	くすり	【N】	medicine; drug	くすりを のみます。
22.	(お)さけ	【N】	alcoholic beverage; liquor; sake (Japanese rice wine)	あまり おさけを 飲みません。
23.	そと	【N】	outside; outdoors	そとへ でましょうか。
24.	みち	【N】	road; street; direction (how to go)	みちは ひろいです。 みちを おしえて 下さい。
25.	ちず	【N】	map	ちずを 見ましょう。
26.	きそく	【N】	rule; regulation	いろいろな きそくが あります。
27.	こえ	【N】	voice	かれは こえが ひくいです。
*28.	こたえ	【N】	answer [STEM OF kotae-masu]	こたえが 分かりません。
29.	タクシー	【N】	taxi	タクシーで 行きましょう。
*30.	テープレコーダー	【N】	tape recorder	テープレコーダーを 買います。
31.	ほか (の + NOUN)	【N】	(an)other...; ...else	ほかの 人に 聞いて 下さい。
	ほか (に + VERB)		besides that	ほかに 何か 言いましたか。
32.	たかはし	【N】	Takahashi [SURNAME]	
33.	きみ	【Pron】	you [INFORMAL, USED BY MEN TO PEOPLE OF THEIR OWN AGE AND YOUNGER]	きみ、だいじょうぶ？
*34.	あさって	【N,Ad】	day after tomorrow	あしたか あさって 行きます。
35.	おおきな 〜	【Pren】	big; large [SAME MEANING AS ookii, BUT APPEARS ONLY BEFORE NOUNS]	大きな こえで 話して います。
36.	しずかに	【Ad】	quietly [ADVERBIAL FORM OF shizuka]	しずかに あるきましょう。
37.	NOUN いん	【Suf】	...employee; ...member	かいしゃいん、ぎんこういん、としょかんいん
38.	TIME いない	【Suf】	...or less	きかんは 二週間 いないです。
39.	TIME いご	【Suf】	...or thereafter	一月 九日 いごに 来て 下さい。
40.	すると	【Conj】	then; thereupon	私は ねて いました。 すると、としょかんいんが 来ました。

Expression:

a. SENTENCE って。 "He/She said that..." = ...と (言って いました IS OMITTED.)

Translation of the Examples:

1. Please come by five o'clock.
Rev. Please wait until five o'clock.
2. I heard the story from my friend.
3. I'll borrow the book from my friend.
4. I'll lend the book to my friend.
5. I'll check and see.
6. The letter was returned.
7. You should rest, o.k.?
   I missed school today.
8. I woke my child up.
Rev. My child woke up.
Rev. I spent a lot of money.
9. Please take out your notebook.
   I turned in my homework.
   I mailed the letter.
10. ① to take... out, to borrow/check... out
    ② It started to rain.
11. We can lend it (to you).
12. I'll dine in the hotel.
13. The meeting will start.
14. I'll use this typewriter.
15. There is some homework.
16. I exercise every day.
17. The (lending, etc.) period is three days.
18. last term, this term, next term
19. How was your New Year's Day?
20. I might become a doctor.
21. I take medicine.
22. I don't drink much.
23. Shall we go outside?
24. The streets are wide.
    Please tell me how to get there.
25. Let's look at the map.
26. There are various regulations.
27. His voice is low (pitched).
28. I don't know the answer.
29. Let's go by taxi.
30. I'll buy a tape recorder.
31. Please ask other people (OR someone else).
    Did he/she say anything else (OR besides that)?
33. Are you o.k.?
34. I'll go either tomorrow or the day after.
35. They are talking in a loud (Lit. big) voice.
36. Let's walk quietly.
37. company employee, bank employee, librarian
38. The (lending, etc.) period is two weeks or less.
39. Please come on January 9th or after.
40. I was sleeping.
    Then the librarian came.

だい十四かの ぶんぽう

I. VERB-ても いいです and VERB-ては いけません

Permission: VERB-ても いいです。 "You may do..." "It is allowed/o.k. to do..." "I permit you to do..."

VERB-ても かまいません。 "I don't mind/care if you do..."
[SAME MEANING AS ABOVE, BUT POLITER]

Prohibition: VERB-ては いけません。 "You may/must not do..." "It is not allowed/o.k. to do..." "I forbid you to do..."

Exchanges with these expressions occur between someone who has the authority to grant the permission and the person asking for it. Notice that the particle mo is used in the affirmative (Lit. "Doing... is also o.k.") while wa is used in the negative (Lit. "Doing... will not do"). The particle yo is often added at the end of the answers.

1. a. 行っても いいですよ。 "You may go."
   b. 行っては いけませんよ。 "You may not (OR must not) go."

2. 学生： 英語で 話しても いいですか。 "May I speak in English?"
   先生1： ええ、(英語で 話しても) いいですよ。 "Yes, you may (speak in Eng.)."
   先生2： いいえ、(英語で 話しては) いけませんよ。 "No, you may not (speak in English)."

Kamai-masen is negative in its form, but affirmative in its meaning. Just think of this as the politer counterpart of ii desu.

3. A: この ざっしを 読んでも かまいませんか。 "Do you mind if read this magazine?"
   B1: ええ、(読んでも) かまいませんよ。 "No, I don't mind (if you read it)." OR "Sure, you can read it."
   SOMETIMES MORE APPROPRIATE TO SAY:
   B2: ええ、どうぞ 読んで 下さい。 "Sure, please feel free to read it."

4. A: タバコを すっては いけませんか。 "May I not smoke?" OR "Is it bad if I smoke?"
   B1: ええ、(すっては) いけませんよ。 "That's right. You may not (smoke)."
   B2: ええ、すわない 方が いいですよ。 "Right. It's better if you don't."
   B3: いいえ、(すっても) いいですよ。 "No, you may (smoke)."
   B4: いいえ、(すっても) かまいませんよ。 SAME AS B-3, BUT POLITER
   B5: いいえ、どうぞ すって 下さい。 "No, please feel free to smoke."

QUESTIONS WITH ...n desu ka (OR ne) ASK FOR A CONFIRMATION OF WHAT ONE ASSUMES:

5. A: 車を 買っても いいんですか。 "You mean I can buy a car?"
   B: ええ、いいですよ。 "Yes, you may."

6. A: アルバイトを やめては いけないんですね。 "(That means) I can't quit my part-time job, right?"
   B: ええ、いけません。 "That's right. You may not."

7. Reading Comprehension Passage (p.169):

   ...わたしは「ねるのも いけないんですか。」と きいた。 としょかんいんは 「ねるのは かまいませんが、しずかに ねて ください。」と いった。

   "... 'Is it that sleeping (here) is also forbidden?' I asked. The librarian said, 'I don't mind your sleeping (itself), but please sleep quietly.'"

Here the dictionary form is used with ikenai and kamaimasen instead of the -te form because the writer is not seeking permission from the librarian, but is simply asking what the general rules of the library are. Notice also that the use of mo "also" and wa (for contrast) is contrary to the foregoing discussion.

Starting with Lesson 13, the reading comprehension passages are written in the plain style. It is more common for diaries, novels, scholarly essays, newspaper articles, etc. to be written with the plain style endings, while letters, speeches, etc. are usually written with the polite style endings.

II. The Tense in 'toki'-Clauses   cf. L.13. VI.

When a toki-clause expresses an action (or event), the verb must be in the PAST tense form if that action precedes the action of the main clause. (This will be discussed in greater detail in L.23.) When a toki-clause expresses a state, it can be in the present tense regardless of whether the main clause is in present or past.

1. おなかが すいた 時は りんごを 食べます。 "When I get (OR have gotten) hungry, I eat an apple."
   PAST

2. おそく なった 時は バスで かえります。 "When I get (OR have gotten) late, I go home by bus."
   PAST

3. あたまが いたい 時は くすりを のみます。 "When I have a headache, I take medicine."
   PRESENT

4. 分からない 時は 友だちに 聞きます。 "When I don't understand, I ask my friend."
   PRESENT

III. CLAUSE (X) ば、CLAUSE (Y)   "If X, then Y."

Ba is one of several particles that marks "hypothetical" clauses in Japanese. When it is preceded by a verb, the main clause should be a factual statement, not a request, proposal, etc. Ba goes particularly well with potential verbs, "can do...," and naru, "become," in the main clause.

(A) The ba Form of Verbs

The rule of ba form construction applies to all groups of verbs: change the final syllable ...u into ...e and add ba.

u-Verbs: のむ → のめば、 はなす → はなせば、 いそぐ → いそげば...
ru-Verbs: いる → いれば、 やめる → やめれば、 でかける → でかければ...
Irregular Verbs: くる → くれば、 する → すれば

1. この 本を 読めば、すぐ 分かりますよ。   "If you read this book, you'll understand right away."
2. 毎日 テニスを すれば、だれでも じょうずに なります。   "Anybody will be good at tennis if he plays it every day."
3. この きかいを つかえば、はやいかも しれません。   "If you use this machine, it might be quick."

As far as u-verbs are concerned, the syllabary chart below is useful in remembering their conjugation because each row represents a different form. Change the final syllable of an u-verb along the column to obtain appropriate form. In the chart below, wa appears in place of a, and some columns are omitted from the regular chart:

ら	ま	ば	な	た	さ	か	わ	+ ない	= Plain, Negative Form
り	み	び	に	ち	し	き	い	+ ます	= -masu Form
る	む	ぶ	ぬ	つ	す	く	う		= Dictionary Form
れ	め	べ	ね	て	せ	け	え	+ ば	= ba Form
ろ	も	ぼ	の	と	そ	こ	お	+ う	= Volitional Form

Plain, Neg.:	とらない	あそばない	しなない	またない	きかない	あわない
-masu Form:	とります	あそびます	しにます	まちます	ききます	あいます
Dict. Form:	とる	あそぶ	しぬ	まつ	きく	あう
ba Form:	とれば	あそべば	しねば	まてば	きけば	あえば
Vol. Form:	とろう	あそぼう	しのう	まとう	きこう	あおう

(B) VERB ば いいんです   "All one has to do is..." "You only need to do..."
Lit. "If one does..., then it will be good."

This is a set phrase offering a solution for a problem. Memorize the question, Doo sure ba ii desu ka (Lit. "If one does how, will it be good?") as "What should one do?"

- 105 -

4. A: かぜを ひいた 時は どう すれば　　"What do you suppose one should do when
　　　いいでしょうか。　　　　　　　　　　one has caught a cold?"

　　B1: びょういんへ 行けば いいんです。　"All one has to do is go to the clinic."
　　　　　　　　　　　　　　　　　　　　　OR "You should go to the clinic."

When there are two or more actions to be taken, combine the verbs using the -te form; only the last verb takes the ba form.

　　B2: くすりを のんで、よく 休めば いい　"All one has to do is take medicine and
　　　　んです。　　　　　　　　　　　　　rest well."

(C) The ba Form of i-Adjectives and 'nai'

The ba form of i-adjectives and nai (all the negative forms) is obtained by changing the final i into kere ba. There is, however, no ba form for the affirmative form of the copula (noun/na-adjective + da).

5. a. 安ければ 買います。　　　　　　　　"If it's cheap, I'll buy it."

　　b. 安く なければ 買いません。　　　　"If it's not cheap, I won't buy it."
　　　　　　　　　　　　　　　　　　　　OR "Unless it's cheap, I won't buy it."

6. a. 良い しごとじゃ なければ しません。"If it's not a good job, I won't do it."

　　b. 良い しごとが なければ 大学いんへ　"If I can't find (Lit. there isn't) a
　　　　行きます。　　　　　　　　　　　　good job, I'll go to graduate school."

7. ごはんを 食べなければ 大きく なりませんよ。"If you don't eat, you won't grow."

8. 今 べんきょう しなければ あとで こまります "If I don't study now, I'll be in
　　ね。　　　　　　　　　　　　　　　　　trouble later, won't I?"

IV. VERB (PRES.) はずです　　"He/She is supposed to do..."
　　　　　　　　　　　　　　"SOMETHING should (I expect will) HAPPEN."

Hazu is a noun which must be always preceded by its modifier. It indicates the speaker's personal expectation or strong belief. Like deshoo, it cannot be used with a speaker's intentional actions, e.g., "I'm supposed to read this book by tomorrow." Neither can it be used to indicate a social norm, e.g., "Students are supposed to study."

1. ひこうきは 四時に つく はずです。　"The plane is supposed to arrive at 4."
　　　　　　　　　　　　　　　　　　　OR "The plane should arrive at four."

2. A: きょうとで とった しゃしんは いつ　"When will the pictures you took in
　　　できるんですか。　　　　　　　　　Kyoto come out?"

　　B: 来週の 月よう日に できる はずです。"They're supposed to come out next
　　　　　　　　　　　　　　　　　　　　　Monday."

3. A: えいが(は) まだ はじまりませんね。 "The movie hasn't started yet, has it?"
   B: ええ、もう はじまる はずなんですが、 "No, it's supposed to have started
      どう したんでしょう(か)。 already, but I wonder what happened."
   A: きいて みましょうか。 "Shall I ask to find out?"
   B: ええ、きいて みて 下さい。 "Yes, please."

V. DIRECT OBJECT (X) は SUBJECT (Y) が VERB   "As for X, Y does/did..."

In this pattern, the original direct object is the topic, and the emphasis is on what has happened or what is going to happen to it. In regular sentences, however, the actor subject is usually the topic, and the emphasis is on what he/she does.

1. あさごはんは しゅじんが つくります。 "As for breakfast, my HUSBAND makes it."
cf. しゅじんは あさごはんを つくります。 "My husband makes BREAKFAST."

In the first example above, the speaker is talking about "breakfast," not what "her husband" does. In fact, shujin is not expected to be brought up by the listener, and therefore it is marked by the particle ga for new information instead of wa for shared information or contrast.

2. A: きのう もらった おさけは どこですか。 "Where's the liquor I got yesterday?"
   B: ああ、あれは (OR あの おさけは) 今 "Oh, that (OR that liquor), Mr.
      よしださんが 飲んで いますよ。 Yoshida is drinking it now."
3. A: この しょうせつは だれが 書いたんですか。 "Who wrote this novel?"
   B: なつめ そうせきだと 思います。 "I think it's by Natsume Soseki."

VI. The Particles 'made ni' and 'ni'

1. a. 火よう日までに かえって 来ます。 "I'll be back by Tuesday." [DEADLINE]
   cf. 火よう日まで ロサンゼルスに います。 "I'll be in L.A. until Tuesday."
   b. その てがみは あしたまでに 書こうと "As for that letter, I'm planning to
      思って います。 write it by tomorrow."
2. りょうしんに お金を かりました。 "I borrowed money from my parents."
      (OR から) [SOURCE]
cf. 友だちに お金を かしました。 "I lent money to my friend."
      (NOT から) [INDIRECT OBJECT]

だい十五かの あたらしい ことば

1. (Xを) つれて いく 【VPhr】 to take (PERSON/ANIMAL) along
   [tsureru "be with" + iku]　子どもを つれて 行きます。

*2. (Xを) つれて くる 【VPhr】 to bring (PERSON/ANIMAL) along
    [tsureru + kuru]　子どもを つれて 来ます。

*3. (Xを) もって いく 【VPhr】 to take (THING) along　かさを もって 行きます。

*4. (Xを) もって くる 【VPhr】 to bring (THING) along　かさを もって 来ます。
    [motsu + iku/kuru]

5. (Xが) いらっしゃる 【u-V】 to go; come; be (exist)　先生は いらっしゃいます。
   [POLITE FOR -- iku, kuru, iru]

6. (Xが) きまる 【u-V】 (for X) to be decided
   きまって いる [STATE]　to be (already) decided　時間は きまって います。

*7. (うたを) うたう 【u-V】 to sing (songs)　うたを うたって 下さい。

8. (Xに Yを) おくる 【u-V】 to send/ship (Y to X)　友だちに 本を おくります。

9. (Xに) でる 【ru-V】 to appear (in/on X)　ゆうべ テレビに でました。

10. かいもの 【VN】 shopping　かいものに 行きましょう。

11. あんない 【VN】 guide; information
    PLACE へ ～する　to guide; show (to...)　ならへ あんない します。
    PLACE を ～する　to show...　ならを あんない します。

12. はなみ 【VN】 flower viewing　あした はなみに 行きます。
    [USUALLY CHERRY BLOSSOMS, hana "flower" + mi(masu)]

13. けんきゅう 【VN】 research　れきしの けんきゅうを します。
    けんきゅうしつ 【N】 professor's office [kenkyuu + shitsu "...room"]

14. しょうかい 【VN】 introduction
    (Xに Yを) ～する　to introduce (Y to X)　りょうしんに みちこさんを
    　　　　　　　　　　　　　　　　　　　　しょうかい しました。

15. ごちそう 【VN】 feast; fine dishes
    ～する　to treat to a meal　今日は ごちそう しますよ。

16. はな 【N】 flower　きれいな はなですね。

17. おとうと 【N】 younger brother　おとうとが ひとり います。

18. いもうと 【N】 younger sister　いもうとは いません。
    [otooto/imooto-san FOR OTHER'S BROTHERS & SISTERS]

19. たんじょうび 【N】 birthday　(お)たんじょう日は いつですか。

20. おくりもの 【N】 present　おくりものを 買いに 行きます。
    [okuri(masu) + mono]

*21. たべもの 【N】 food　食べものを 売っています。

- 108 -

*22.	のみもの	【N】	drink	飲みものは たりますか。
23.	にんぎょう	【N】	doll	にんぎょうを つくりました。
	にほん にんぎょう	【N】	Japanese doll in kimono	
24.	うた	【N】	song	その うたを しって います。
25.	おんがくかい (OR おんがっかい)	【N】	concert [ongaku + kai "gathering"]	おんがく会の きっぷが あります。
26.	まんが	【N】	cartoon; comics	ときどき まんがを 読みます。
27.	こうくうびん	【N】	airmail	こうくうびんで だしました。
*28.	しゅみ	【N】	hobby	しゅみは 何ですか。
29.	しけん	【N】	examination	かがくの しけんが あります。
*30.	きまつ	【N】	end of the term [ki (as in gak-ki) + matsu (as in shuu-matsu)]	きまつしけんは むずかしそうです。
*31.	しょうがっこう	【N】	elementary school (1st-6th grades)	
*32.	ちゅうがっこう	【N】	middle/junior high school (7th-9th grades)	
*33.	カメラ	【N】	camera	友だちに カメラを もらいました。
34.	ヨーロッパ	【N】	Europe	ヨーロッパへ 行くよていです。
35.	もりた よしこ	【N】	Yoshiko Morita [Yoshiko IS A FEMALE GIVEN NAME]	
36.	いくつ（ですか）	【N】	how old [QW FOR AGE]	おばあさんは おいくつですか。
*37.	NUMBER さい	【Suf】	...years old [AGE]	六十五さいです。
38.	かわいい	【i-A】	cute	かわいい にんぎょうですね。
39.	(Xが) ほしい	【i-A】	want X (something)	私は とけいが ほしいです。
*40.	(Xが) きらい(な)	【na-A】	dislike; hate X	私は さかなが きらいです。
41.	とても	【Ad】	very... [= taihen]	とても うれしいです。
*42.	いちばん	【Ad】	the most... [Lit. "number one"]	一ばん 大きい まちです。
43.	まえに	【Ad】	before; previously [NOUN + ni]	前に 一ど かのじょに 会いました。
44.	だい (すき/きらい)	【Pref】	(like/hate) very much	やきゅうが 大すきです。

Expression:

a. でも、それじゃ...　"But in that case..."
　　("I'd be asking you too much" OR "I'd feel bad" IS OMITTED)

b. いいんです。　"It's o.k." [IN THE SENSE, "Please don't worry about it."]

Numbers and Counters:

〜さい/〜つ: ...years old. For a complete list of ...<u>tsu</u>, see L.7, p.46.

	1: いっさい	2: にさい	3: さんさい	...	10: じっさい	11: じゅういっさい
OR	ひとつ	ふたつ	みっつ		とお	じゅういち

	15: じゅうごさい	20: にじっさい	...	30: さんじっさい	...	なんさい "how old"
OR	じゅうご	はたち		さんじゅう		いくつ

Translation of the Examples:

1. I'll take my child with me.
2. I'll bring my child here.
3. I'll take my umbrella with me.
4. I'll bring my umbrella here.
5. The teacher goes (OR comes OR is there).
6. The time is set (OR has been decided).
7. Please sing a song.
8. I'll send a book to my friend.
9. I was on television last night.
10. Let's go shopping.
11. I'll take him to Nara.
    I'll show him around Nara.
12. I'll go flower-viewing tomorrow.
13. I'll do research on history.
14. I introduced Michiko to my parents.
15. I'll treat you today.
16. Pretty flower, isn't it?
17. I have one younger brother.
18. I don't have a younger sister.
19. When is your birthday?
20. I'm going (in order) to buy a gift.
21. They sell food (there).
22. Is there enough to drink?
23. I made a doll.
24. I know that song.
25. I have tickets to a concert.
26. I read comic books sometimes.
27. I mailed it airmail.
28. What's your hobby?
29. There is a science examination.
30. The final examination seems difficult.
33. I received a camera from my friend.
34. I plan to go to Europe.
36. How old is your grandmother (OR the old lady)?
37. She is 65 years old.
38. Cute doll, isn't it?
39. I want a watch.
40. I hate fish.
41. I'm very glad.
42. It's the biggest city.
43. I met her once before.
44. I like baseball very much.
OR I love baseball.

だい十五かの ぶんぽう

I. NOUN が すきです　　　　　　　"like SOMETHING; enjoy SOMETHING"
　　VERB (DICT.) のが すきです　　"like to do... ; enjoy doing..."
　　　　　　　　　　　　　　　　　cf. L.11, I. and L.12, I.

　　No is attached to the dictionary form of a verb to make it into a noun (L.12, V.). Use kirai(na), in place of suki(na), to mean "dislike; hate."

1. 私は えいが (を みるの) が すきです。　　　　　"I like (to see) movies."
　　　　　　　すきじゃ ありません。　　　　　　　　"I don't like..."
　　　　　　　すきでした。　　　　　　　　　　　　"I used to like..."
　　　　　　　すきじゃ ありませんでした。　　　　　"I didn't like..."

2. 田中さんは おんがくを 聞くのが すきなんです。　"It's that..."
　　...すきだと 思います。　　　　　　　　　　　　"I think that..."
　　...すきで、よく レコードを 買います。　　　　"Ms. Tanaka likes to listen to music, and (so) she buys records often."

3. A: しゅみは 何ですか。　　　　　　　　　　　　"What's your hobby?"
　　B: いろいろな ところへ 行って、しゃしんを とる　"I like going to various
　　　 のが すきです。　　　　　　　　　　　　　　 places and taking pictures."

4. 高校の 時、しょうせつを 読むのは 大すきでしたが、"When I was in high school,
　　べんきょうを するのは あまり すきじゃ ありません　I loved to read novels,
　　でした。[THE PARTICLE wa IS USED FOR CONTRAST]　but I didn't like to study
　　　　　　　　　　　　　　　　　　　　　　　　　 very much."

5. 私は しゅくだいを するのが きらいです。　　　　"I hate (to do) homework."

6. [うたを うたうのが きらいな] 人は もりさんです。"The person who hates to sing (songs) is Mr. Mori."

7. [つりに 行くのが すきだった] 人は 川上さんです。"The person who liked to go fishing was Mr. Kawakami."

　　Suki (and kirai) must be used in general terms, and not for a one-time experience. For example, to ask a question such as "Did you like the movie last night?" you should say, Yuube no eega wa yokatta desu ka "Was the movie last night good?," not suki deshita ka, which means "Did you used to like...?"

II. NOUN が ほしいです　　　　　"I/You want SOMETHING."
　　NOUN を ほしがって います　　"He/She/They want(s) SOMETHING."

　　These patterns are used to express that one wants "something," but it cannot be used for wanting "to do" something. Hoshii is an i-type adjective

- 111 -

and it is used with first- and second-person subjects. With third-person subjects, the suffix -garu (or its stative form, -gatte iru) is attached to the stem hoshi. Notice that the particle ga is used with hoshii, while o is used with hoshi-garu/-gatte iru.

The distinction is derived from the idea that one can feel and express one's own feelings and ask about the addressee's feelings, but cannot feel another's. -Gatte iru indicates that the speaker is objectively stating that a third person is showing a sign of his/her feelings or desires. (This suffix is also used with other i-adjectives expressing feelings, such as ureshii and samui.) One can use it when referring to one's own family members, close friends and children, but when referring to others, it is more appropriate to say, "someone says he feels/wants..." or "someone seems to feel/want..."

1. 私は 車 が ほしいです。 "I want a car."
　　　　　ほしく ありません。 "I don't want a car."
　　　　　ほしかったです。 "I wanted a car."
　　　　　ほしく ありませんでした。 "I didn't want a car."

2. 子どもは ねこ を ほしがって います。 "My child wants a cat."
　　ほしがって いません。～いました。～いませんでした。

3. 良い じしょが ほしかったので、えきの 前の 本やへ 行って みました。 "I wanted a good dictionary, so I tried (going to) the bookstore in front of the station."

4. [私が 今 ほしい] もの は テープレコーダーです。 "What (The thing that) I want now is a tape recorder."

5. [いもうとが ほしがって いる] ふくは 高そうです。 "The dress that my younger sister wants looks expensive."

Hoshii desu straightforwardly expresses one's desire. In contrast, hoshii to omoimasu (Lit. I think I want...) corresponds to the English expression, "I would like...," which is an indirect way of expressing it and sounds more polite.

6. A: たんじょう日に 何が ほしいと 思いますか。 "What would you like on your birthday?"
　 B: あたらしい タイプが ほしいと 思います。 "I would like a new typewriter."
　 A: そうですか。私の おとうとも タイプを ほしがって いるんですよ。 "Is that right? My younger brother wants a typewriter, too."

It is rude to ask someone hoshii desu ka (or hoshii to omoimasu ka) when you are offering something. For example, when you want to say, "Do you want some tea?" you should say, "O-cha, nomimasu ka" or more politely, "O-cha wa ikaga desu ka."

III. VERB (STEM) たいです   "I/You want to do..."
    VERB (STEM) たがって います   "He/She/They want(s) to do..."

For "wanting to do something," ...tai is used with first- and second-person subjects, while ...ta-gatte iru is used with third-person subjects. Tai is a suffix (an i-type adjective) that is attached to the STEM of a verb. (Be careful not to confuse this with the past tense form of a verb.) -Garu is attached to its stem, -ta. The direct object of a verb sometimes can be marked by ga with -tai, but always by o with -ta-gatte iru. Again, ...tai to omoimasu "I would like to do..." sounds indirect and polite.

1. 私(わたし)は うちへ かえり<u>たい</u>です。   "I want to go home."
   かえり<u>たく ありません</u>。   "I don't want to go home."
   かえり<u>たかったです</u>。   "I wanted to go home."
   かえり<u>たく ありませんでした</u>。   "I didn't want to go home."

2. 子(こ)どもは ピアノを ならい<u>たがって います</u>。   "My child wants to take piano lessons."

     ならい<u>たがって いません</u>。〜<u>いました</u>。〜<u>いませんでした</u>。

3. A: 日本(にほん)では 何(なに)を (OR が) し<u>たい</u>と 思(おも)いますか。   "What would you like to do in Japan?"
   B: きょうとへ 行(い)って、いろいろな おてらを (OR が) 見(み)<u>たい</u>と 思(おも)います。   "I'd like to go to Kyoto and see various temples."
   A: そうですか。 ミラーさんも きょうとへ 行(い)き<u>たがって います</u>よ。   "Is that right? Ms. Miller wants to go to Kyoto, too."

4. 中国(ちゅうごく)の 文学(ぶんがく)を べんきょう し<u>たい</u>と 思(おも)って、この 大学(だいがく)へ 来(き)ました。   "I wanted to study Chinese literature, and (so) I came to this university."

5. きのうは はが いたくて、何(なに)も 食(た)べ<u>たく ありませんでした</u>。   "Yesterday I had a toothache and didn't want to eat anything."

6. A: [一(いち)ばん 行(い)き<u>たい</u>] 国(くに)は どこですか。   "What (Where) is the country you want to go to the most?"
   B: イギリスです。   "It's Great Britain."

7. [おとうとが 会(あ)い<u>たがって いる</u>] 人(ひと)は みち子(こ)さんです。   "The person whom my younger brother wants to meet is Michiko."

To ask ...tai desu ka is also rude when you are offering something or inviting someone to do something with you. For example, when you want to say, "Do you want to come to my house?" it is more appropriate to say, <u>Uchi e kimasen ka</u> (Lit. "Won't you come to my house?").

IV. VERB (PAST AFF.) ことが あります   "have done... (in the past); have had the experience of doing..."

...Ta koto ga arimasu literally means, "There are occasions when one has done..." Referring to a past action at a specific time, use VERB-mashita.

1. A: おすしを 食^たべた ことが ありますか。 "Have you EVER eaten sushi?"
   B: ええ、あります。 / いいえ、ありません。 "Yes, I have. / No, I haven't."

cf. a. きのう おすしを 食べましたか。 "Did you eat sushi yesterday?"
   b. A: もう ひるごはんを 食べましたか。 "Have you eaten lunch yet?"
      B1: ええ、食べました。 "Yes, I have."
      B2: いいえ、まだ 食べて いません。 "No, I haven't yet."

2. A: 山本さんという 人を しって いますか。 "Do you know (of) the man named Yamamoto?"
   B: 名前は 聞いた ことが ありますが、会った ことは ありません。 "I've heard the name, but never met him." [wa FOR CONTRAST]

3. A: 日本語で 手紙を 書いた ことが ありますか。 "Have you ever written a letter in Japanese?"
   B: いいえ、まだ ないんです。書いて みたいと 思いますが。 "No, not yet. I'd like to try (writing one), though."

V. VERB (PRES.) つもりです   "I intend to do..." "I plan to do..."

Tsumori is a noun which must be always preceded by its modifier. This pattern expresses the speaker's intention; therefore, to indicate someone else's intention, you must add, "He/She says" or "I hear that..." Compared to ...yotee desu, it sounds more subjective and tentative, similar to VERB (VOL.) to omotte imasu.

1. 今年の 五月に ロンドンへ 行く つもりです。 "I intend to go to London this May." OR "My intention is to go..."

cf. a. ... 行く よていです。 "I am/He is scheduled to go..." "My/His plan is to go..."
    b. ... 行こうと 思って います。 "I'm thinking of going..." "I'm planning to..."
    c. ... 行くと 思います。 "I think I/he will go..." [BUT I'M NOT SURE]
    d. ... 行くかも しれません。 "I/He might go..."
    e. ... 行くでしょう。 "He/She will probably go..." [NOT 'I']
    f. ... 行く はずです。 "He/She is supposed to go..." [NOT 'I']
    g. ... 行きます。 "I am/He is going..." "I/He will go..."

2. あした ジョンソンさんに でんわを かけて、　　"I intend to call Mr. Johnson
　　きいて みる <u>つもり</u>です。　　　　　　　　　　tomorrow and ask him."

3. A: 車を 買うんですか。　　　　　　　　　　　　"You're going to buy a car?"

　　B: ええ、まだ よく 分かりませんが、小さい 車を　　"Yes, I'm not sure yet, but I
　　　　買う <u>つもり</u>です。　　　　　　　　　　　　intend to buy a small car."

VI. ...なので vs. ...だから　　"because (it) is..."

Both <u>kara</u> and <u>no de</u> can be preceded by the plain form. One exception is that the <u>plain present affirmative</u> form of the copula (NOUN/na-ADJ <u>da</u>) must be replaced by <u>na</u> before <u>no de</u>. The situation is the same preceding <u>n(o) desu</u>.

1. あさっては かのじょの たんじょうび<u>なので</u>、　　"Since the day after tomorrow is
　　　　　　　　　　(OR ～<u>だから</u>)　　　　　　my girlfriend's birthday, I'm
　　どこかへ つれて 行こうと 思って います。　　　　planning to take her somewhere."

2. この じしょは べんり<u>なので</u>、みんなが つかって　"This dictionary is handy, so
　　います。 (OR べんり<u>だから</u>)、　　　　　　　　everyone uses it."

cf. a. Pres. Neg.: この じしょは べんり<u>じゃ ないので</u>、だれも つかいません。
　　　　　　　　　　(OR べんり<u>じゃ ないから</u>)

　　b. Past Aff.: おとといは ひま<u>だったので</u>、えいがを 見に 行きました。
　　　　　　　　　　(OR ひま<u>だったから</u>)

　　c. Pres. Aff. (i-ADJ): 今日は さむ<u>いので</u>、一日中 りょうに いる つもりです。
　　　　　　　　　　(OR さむ<u>いから</u>)

　　d. A: どうして テニスを しないんですか。　　"Why don't you play tennis?"

　　　　B: とても へた<u>なんです</u>。　　　　　　　　"I'm very bad at it. That's why."

VII. Polite Expressions　(To be discussed in greater detail in L.19 and L.22.)

(A) いらっしゃる: Honorific Form of 行く、来る、いる

Honorific forms are used to describe the actions or belongings of one's "superiors" (i.e., others who are older and/or higher in rank), but never for oneself or one's own family members. <u>Irassharu</u> is conjugated like an <u>u</u>-verb, except for the -<u>masu</u> form, which is <u>irasshai-masu</u> instead of <u>irasshari-masu</u>.

1. A: いとう先生は <u>いらっしゃいますか</u>。　　　　"Is Prof. Ito in?"
　　　　　　　　　　(います)

　　B: ちょっと ぎんこうへ <u>いらっしゃいましたけど</u>、"He went to the bank (for a
　　　　　　　　　　　　　(行きました)　　　　　　little while), but I think
　　すぐ <u>もどって いらっしゃる</u>と 思います。　　he'll be right back."
　　　　(もどって 来る)

2. A: ごりょうしんは どこに <u>すんで</u> <u>いらっしゃいますか</u>。　"Where do your parents
　　　　　　　　　　（すんで います）　　　　　　　　　　　　live?"
   B: テキサスに すんで います。(NOT いらっしゃいます)　"They live in Texas."

(B) More on Prefixes 'o-' and 'go-'

<u>O-</u> + VERBAL NOUN (usually of Japanese origin)/VERB STEM + <u>desu</u> is an honorific expression describing the actions of one's superior or of the addressee when one is being polite.

1. <u>お</u>かいもの<u>ですか</u>。　　　　　　　　　　　"Are you shopping?"
2. ご主人は いつ <u>お</u>かえり<u>でしょうか</u>。　　　"When do you expect your husband to be back?"
3. A: どちらへ <u>お</u>でかけ<u>ですか</u>。　　　　　　"Where are you going (out)?"
   B: ちょっと そこまで...　　　　　　　　Lit. "As far as over there for a moment."

Example 3 is a very common exchange between neighbors or acquaintances in Japan, almost as a way of greeting. The questioner is not necessarily trying to find out where the other party is going, and therefore the response above is quite appropriate.

<u>Go-</u> + VERBAL NOUN (of Chinese origin) + <u>shimasu</u> is a humble expression, referring to one's own (and one's family's) actions for or to one's superior. They are also used when the speaker is simply being polite to the addressee in describing his/her own action.

4. A: きょうとへ <u>ご</u>あんない <u>しましょうか</u>。　"Shall I (humbly) take (Lit. guide) you to Kyoto?"
   B: ええ、おねがい します。　　　　　　　"Yes, please." Lit. "I (humbly) request/wish it."
5. 先生に 高校の 時の 友だちを <u>ご</u>しょうかい <u>しました</u>。　"I (humbly) introduced my high school friend to my teacher."

VIII. Some Notes on the Stems of Verbs

Verbs become nouns in their stem forms. Stems can combine with other nouns to form compounds.

1. やすみ "vacation," はなし "talk; story," あそび "game," こたえ "answer," はじめ "the beginning," おわり "the end," かしだし "lending service"...
2. 食べもの "food," 飲みもの "drink," たてもの "building"(たてます "to build"), おくりもの "gift" (おくります "to send"), きもの "Japanese traditional robe" (きます "to wear") cf. かいもの "shopping" (NOT "things bought")

APPENDIX 1: SUMMARY OF PARTICLE USAGE

I. Grammatical Particles

1. NOUN が

a. Subject when it is emphasized and the predicate is understood (e.g., as an answer to, "Who is going?"): 私が 行きます。

b. Subject when the whole event is newly presented: りょうしんが たずねて 来たんです。

c. Subject that is a question word: 何が ありますか。

d. Subject of a subordinate clause when it is different from the main clause subject: これは [子どもが 見る] えいがです。

e. Subject of the comment clause in 'A wa B ga C':
（私は）山下さんが 来なくて ざんねんです。
スミスさんは せいが たかいです。

f. Direct object with potential verbs: よしゅうが できませんでした。

g. Direct object with hoshii (and VERB-tai): 私は ねこが ほしいです。

2. NOUN を

a. Direct object: 本を 読みます。

b. Place of motion: こうえんを あるきます。

3. NOUN に

a. Indirect object, "to": 友だちに はなを 上げました。

b. Target: みち子さんに 会います。

c. Purpose, "for; in order to": あそびに 来て 下さい。

d. Source, "from": 友だちに 車を かりました。

4. NOUN (PLACE) に

a. Place of existing objects, people, and animals, "in; at; on":
ペンは つくえの 上に あります。
ぎんこうに つとめて います。

  b. Destination, "in(to); on(to)": きっさてんに 入(はい)りましょう。

5. NOUN (TIME) に

  a. Specific point in time: まいばん 十二時(じゅうにじ)に ねます。

 cf. ① Time words which take <u>ni</u>: 〜時(じ)、〜分(ふん)、〜月(がつ)、〜日(にち)、〜よう日(び)、休(やす)み...

  ② Time words which do not take <u>ni</u>: あさ、今日(きょう)、毎日(まいにち)、さっき、今週(こんしゅう)、先月(せんげつ)...

  ③ Duration of time does not take <u>ni</u>: 八時間(はちじかん)、一日中(いちにちじゅう)、六時(ろくじ)から 七時(しちじ)まで...

  ④ <u>Ni</u> is optional with time words + <u>goro</u>: 四時(よじ)ごろ、九月(くがつ)ごろ...

  b. Standard of frequency/amount, "per; a": 一日(いちにち)に 三(さん)ど ごはんを 食(た)べます。

6. NOUN (PLACE) へ

  Direction of motion, "to; toward": うちへ かえります。

7. NOUN (PLACE) で

  Place of action, "in; at; on": としょかんで べんきょう します。

8. NOUN で

  a. Means and instrument, "by; with; using": えんぴつで 書(か)きました。

  b. Required time or amount, "within; with": しけんは 五分(ごふん)で はじまります。

    しょうがっきんでは たりません。

9. NOUN の

  a. Noun modification, "...'s": これは 私(わたし)の かさじゃ ありません。

    えきの 前(まえ)の みせで 買(か)いました。

  b. Subject in a noun-modifying clause: ぼくの ならった ことばと ちがいます。
   [INTERCHANGEABLE WITH <u>ga</u>]

10. NOUN と

  a. Partner, "with": 良子(よしこ)さんと でかけます。

  b. Compared object, "(same) as; (different) from": これは あれと おなじです。

c. For joining nouns, "... and ...":　　　　コーヒーと おちゃを 飲みます。

11. NOUN や

   For joining nouns, "..., ..., and so forth":　コーヒーや おちゃを 飲みます。
   [IMPLIES OTHERS NOT MENTIONED]

12. NOUN か

   Alternative, "... or ...":　　　　　　　　　コーヒーか おちゃを 飲みます。

13. NOUN (TIME/PLACE) から

   Starting point, "from":　　　　　　　　　　シカゴから バスで 来ました。

14. NOUN (TIME/PLACE) まで

   Ending point, "to; until":　　　　　　　　来年の 三月まで 日本に います。

15. NOUN (TIME) までに

   Deadline, "by; on or before":　　　　　　仕事は 金よう日までに おわります。

16. NOUN より

   Standard of comparison, "than":　　　　　さかなより にくの 方が すきです。

II. Semantic Particles

17. NOUN (+ PARTICLE) は

   a. Topic (shared information)
      ① Subject (e.g., as an answer to, "Are you going?"):　私は 行きます。
      ② Others (place, time, etc.):　　東京は 今 何時ですか。
      　　　　　　　　　　　　　　　　休みの 日には おそく おきます。
   b. Contrast (e.g., "I won't talk with Mr.
      Tanaka though I will with other people"):　田中さんとは 話しません。

18. NOUN (+ PARTICLE) も

   a. Similarity, "too; also":　　　　いもうとは 学生です。おとうとも 学生です。

   b. Inclusiveness, "both/neither ... and/nor ...":　いもうとも おとうとも います。

III. Sentence Particles

19. SENTENCE か:　　Question:　　きれいですか。　　"Is it pretty?"

20. SENTENCE ね:　　Tag Question: きれいですね。↑　"It's pretty, right?"

21. SENTENCE ね(え): Amazement:　　きれいですね(え)。↓　"How pretty!"

22. SENTENCE よ:　　Emphatic:　　きれいですよ。　"It's pretty, I assure you."

IV. Conjunctive Particles

23. CLAUSE と

　Quotation, "that": 山本さんは 来ると 言って いました。　"Ms. Yamamoto said that she's coming."

24. CLAUSE₁ が、CLAUSE₂　"but"

　良い 天気でしたが、うちに いました。　"It was nice weather, but I stayed home."

25. CLAUSE₁ けれども、CLAUSE₂　"but"

　良い 天気だったけれども、うちに いました。　[SAME MEANING AS 23. ABOVE]

26. CLAUSE₁ から、CLAUSE₂　"so"

　良い 天気だったから、でかけました。　"It was nice weather, so I went out."

27. CLAUSE₁ ので、CLAUSE₂　"so"

　良い 天気だったので、でかけました。　[SAME MEANING AS 25. ABOVE]

28. CLAUSE₁ ば、CLAUSE₂　"if"

　くすりを のめば、元気に なります。　"If you take medicine, you'll get well."

V. Particle Phrases

29. NOUN (X) と いう NOUN (Y)　"Y called X"

　いとうさんと いう 人を 知って いますか。　"Do you know the person named Ito?"

30. NOUN に ついて　"about; concerning"

　せいじに ついて ろんぶんを 書きます。　"I'll write my thesis about politics."

APPENDIX 2: LIST OF COUNTERS

1.	〜じ	"...o'clock"	p. 2
2.	〜えん	"...yen"	p. 7
3.	〜ひゃく/びゃく/ぴゃく	"...hundred"	p. 8
4.	〜せん/ぜん	"...thousand"	p. 8
5.	〜さつ	BOUND OBJECTS	p. 29
6.	〜まい	THIN, FLAT OBJECTS	p. 29
7.	〜ほん/ぼん/ぽん	LONG, CYLINDRICAL OBJECTS	p. 30
8.	〜じかん	"...hours"	p. 30
9.	〜か/にち	"...days" AND DAYS OF THE MONTH	p. 30
10.	〜しゅうかん	"...weeks"	p. 30
11.	〜ねん	"...years" "the year..."	p. 30
12.	〜ど	"...times" [FREQUENCY]	p. 30
13.	〜か	"...lessons" "lesson..."	p. 30
14.	〜ふん/ぷん	"...minutes"	p. 37
15.	〜がつ	NAMES OF THE MONTHS	P. 38
16.	〜つ	ROUND OR CHUNKY OBJECTS	p. 46
17.	〜かげつ	"...months"	p. 46
18.	〜ばん	"number..."	p. 55
19.	〜さい/つ	"...years old"	p.110

Japanese-English Glossary

JAPANESE	KANJI	ENGLISH	LESS. NO.-WORD NO.
		〔あ〕	
ああ		oh	2-34
ああ		in that manner	6-31
アイスクリーム		ice cream	12-32
～あいだ	～間	while	13-31
あう	会う	meet, see	6-03
あおい	青い	blue	2-30
あかい	赤い	red	2-27
あがる	上がる	enter, go up	7-12
あかるい	明るい	bright, light	10-38
あげる	上げる	give	7-16
あさ	朝	morning	1-26
あさって	明後日	day aft. tomor.	14-34
あし	足	foot, leg	13-21
あした	明日	tomorrow	4-39
あそこ		that place	3-38
あそぶ	遊ぶ	play, goof off	8-11
あたま	頭	head	12-16
あたらしい	新しい	fresh, new	6-38
あちら		that way	7-33
あつい	暑い	hot	11-38
あっち		=あちら	11-27
あつめる	集める	collect	13-04
～あと	～後	after...	4-41
あとで	後で	later	8-51
あの～		that...	2-25
あの (う)		Well um...	12-43
アパート		apartment	6-08
あまり		(not) much/often, (not) very...	5-44
あめ	雨	rain	5-12
アメリカ		America	1-04
ある	有る	exist, be	3-43
あるく	歩く	walk	8-10
アルバイト		part-time job	12-14
あれ		that thing	2-21
あんな～		that kind of	5-39
あんない	案内	guide	15-11
いい	良い	good, nice	4-47
いいえ		no	1-11
いう	言う	say	9-05
いかが		how (about)	6-33
いがく	医学	med. science	8-22
イギリス		England	8-26
いく	行く	go	4-08
いくつ	幾つ	how many	7-39
いくつ	幾つ	how old	15-36
いくら	幾ら	how much MONEY	2-31
～いご	以後	...or thereafter	14-39
いしゃ	医者	doctor	14-20
いす	椅子	chair, stool	2-06
いそがしい	忙しい	busy	6-42
いそぐ	急ぐ	hurry	7-07
いたい	痛い	painful	12-35
いち	一	one	1
いちばん	一番	the most	15-42
いつ		when (QW)	7-38
いっしょに	一緒に	together	13-37
いとう	伊藤	NAME	13-24
～いない	以内	...or less	14-38
いぬ	犬	dog	3-25
いま	今	now	1-25
いもうと	妹	younger sister	15-18
いや	嫌	unpleasant	4-48
いらっしゃる		go, come, be POLITE	15-05
いる	居る	exist, be, stay	3-44
いれる	入れる	pour/put into	7-14
いろいろ	色々	various	5-41
いろいろ	色々	in various ways	10-44
～いん	員	...employee	14-37
うえ	上	on, above	3-28
うしろ	後ろ	behind	3-32
うた	歌	song	15-24
うたう	歌う	sing	15-07
うち	家	home, house	4-28
うる	売る	sell	8-12
		noisy	10-40
うれしい	嬉しい	glad, happy	13-32
うん		yeah INFORMAL	13-40
うんどう	運動	exercise	14-16
え (っ)		Pardon?	12-44
えいが	映画	movie	4-25
えいご	英語	English lang.	8-25
ええ		yes	1-10
えき	駅	station	4-31
エレベーター		elevator	3-09
～えん	～円	...yen	2-32
えんぴつ	鉛筆	pencil	2-04
おいしい		delicious	6-40
おおきい	大きい	large, big	6-35
おおきな～	大きな	large, big...	14-35

おかね	お金	money	8-36
おきる	起きる	wake／get up	4-13
おくさん	奥さん	wife POLITE	3-24
おくりもの	贈り物	present	15-20
おくる	送る	send	15-08
おこす	起こす	wake..up	14-08
おじいさん		grandfather, old man	10-23
おしえる	教える	teach, tell	8-13
おそい	遅い	late adj.	4-50
おそく	遅く	late adv.	6-28
おたく	お宅	house POLITE	7-29
おちゃ	お茶	tea	4-23
おとうと	弟	younger brother	15-17
おとこ	男	male	3-17
おとこのこ	男の子	boy	3-19
おとこのひと	男の人 man		3-18
おととい	一昨日	day bef. yest.	5-31
おととし	一昨年	year bef. last	13-30
おなか		stomach	11-14
おなじ	同じ	same	11-42
おばあさん		grandmother, old woman	10-24
おもう	思う	think	9-06
おもしろい	面白い	interesting	7-46
おわる	終わる	end, finish	4-06
おんがく	音楽	music	10-14
おんがくかい	音楽会	concert	15-25
おんな	女	female	3-20
おんなのこ	女の子	girl	3-22
おんなのひと	女の人 woman		3-21

〔か〕

～か	～日	...days, DATE	5
～か	～課	... lessons	5
かいぎ	会議	meeting	14-13
かいしゃ	会社	company	4-30
かいじょう	会場	meeting place	6-09
かいもの	買物	shopping	15-10
かう	買う	buy	5-08
かえる	帰る	return	4-07
かお	顔	face	9-14
かがく	科学	science	8-21
かく	書く	write	8-09
がくせい	学生	student	1-02
かける	掛ける	call PHONE	8-14
かける	掛ける	wear GLASSES	9-07
かさ	傘	umbrella	2-07
(お)かし	お菓子	sweets, snack	10-15
かしだし	貸し出し	lending service	14-11
かす	貸す	lend	14-04
かず	数	number	11-16
かぜ	風邪	cold n.	12-23
がっき	学期	school term	14-18
がっこう	学校	school	2-16
かのじょ	彼女	she	12-34
かばん	鞄	bag, briefcase	2-09
かまう	構う	mind v.	11-11
かまくら	鎌倉	PLACE	11-32
かみ	紙	paper	5-14
かみ(のけ)	髪の毛	hair	12-17
かむ	噛む	bite	12-09
ガム		chewing gum	12-31
カメラ		camera	15-33
かようび	火曜日	Tuesday	4-36
かりる	借りる	borrow	14-03
かれ	彼	he	12-33
かわいい	可愛い	cute	15-38
かわかみ	川上	NAME	8-44
かわく	渇く	get dry	11-04
～かん	～館	BIG BUILDINGS	11-48
かんこく	韓国	Korea	1-06
がんばる	頑張る	try one's best	7-10
きかい	機械	machine	8-38
きかん	期間	period	14-17
きぎょう	企業	enterprise	13-16
きく	聞く	listen, hear, ask	7-01
きそく	規則	rule	14-26
きた	北	north	11-24
ギター		guitar	13-23
きっさてん	喫茶店	coffee shop	3-05
きっぷ	切符	ticket	7-27
きのう	昨日	yesterday	5-30
きまつ	期末	end of term	15-30
きまる	決まる	be decided	15-06
きみ	君	you INFORMAL	14-33
きゃく	客	guest, customer	8-30
きゅう	九	nine	1
きゅうに	急に	suddenly	12-40
きょう	今日	today	4-38
きょうかい	教会	church	4-32
きょうしつ	教室	classroom	3-02
きょうと	京都	PLACE	10-32
きょねん	去年	last year	8-49
きよみずでら	清水寺	TEMPLE	10-33
きらい	嫌い	dislike, hate	15-40
きる	着る	wear	8-08
きれい	綺麗	clean, pretty	6-46
ぎんこう	銀行	bank	3-04
ぎんざ	銀座	PLACE	8-46
きんようび	金曜日	Friday	4-36
く	九	nine	1

くすり	薬	medicine	14-21
くだもの	果物	fruit	7-22
くち	口	mouth	12-21
くつ	靴	shoes	2-10
くつした	靴下	socks	2-11
くに	国	country, hometown	12-25
くらい	暗い	dark	10-39
～ぐらい		about...	5-35
クラス		class	10-26
くる	来る	come	4-15
～てくる	来る	come doing...	12-10
くるま	車	car	8-40
くろい	黒い	black	2-29
けいけん	経験	experience	12-13
けいざい	経済	economy	8-19
けさ	今朝	this morning	9-27
～げつ	月	...month	7-49
けっこん	結婚	marriage	8-16
げつようび	月曜日	Monday	4-36
けれども		however	13-39
げんき	元気	energetic, well	6-48
けんきゅう	研究	research	15-13
けんきゅうしつ	～室	prof.'s office	15-13
ご	五	five	1
～ご	～語	LANGUAGE	1-15
こう		in this manner	6-29
こうえん	公園	park	7-30
こうくうびん	航空便	airmail	15-27
こうこう	高校	high school	5-16
こうはい	後輩	one's junior	9-18
こえ	声	voice	14-27
コーヒー		coffee	3-11
ここ		this place	3-36
ごご	午後	p.m., afternoon	1-24
こころ	心	heart, mind	5-29
ごしゅじん	ご主人	husband POLITE	3-23
ごぜん	午前	a.m.	1-23
こたえ	答	answer n.	14-28
こたえる	答える	answer v.	7-18
ごちそう	御馳走	feast, treat	15-15
こちら		this way	7-31
こちら	〔POLITE〕	this person	8-43
こっち		=こちら	11-25
こと	事	thing, event	5-18
ことし	今年	this year	13-27
ことば	言葉	word, language	10-17
こども	子供	child	3-16
この～		this...	2-23
このあいだ	この間	these days	9-28
このごろ		recently	6-26
こばやし	小林	NAME	6-22
ごはん	御飯	rice, meal	4-21
こまかい（おかね）	細かい	small (change)	8-52
こまる	困る	be at a loss	12-07
こむ	込む	get crowded	11-06
こよう	雇用	employment	13-17
これ		this thing	2-19
これから		from now on	11-46
～ごろ	頃	around...	4-53
こん～	今～	this...	6-52
こんど		this/next time, sometime soon	8-48
こんな～		this kind of	5-37
こんばん	今晩	tonight	4-40

〔さ〕

～さ		...ness	11-49
さあ		well gee...	8-55
～さい	～歳	...years old	15-37
さいご	最後	the end, last	10-30
さいとう	斉藤	NAME	7-37
さいふ	財布	wallet	10-22
さがす	探す	look for	11-07
さかな	魚	fish	6-14
さけ	酒	liquor, sake	14-22
さしあげる	差し～	give HUMBLE	7-17
～さつ	～冊	BOUND OBJECTS	5
さっき		short time ago	8-50
ざっし	雑誌	magazine	4-27
さとう	佐藤	NAME	5-26
さむい	寒い	cold	11-39
さらいしゅう	再来週	week aft.next	13-26
さらいねん	再来年	year aft. next	13-29
サラダ		salad	5-21
～さん		Mr., Ms.--	1-12
さん	三	three	1
さんこうしょ	参考書	reference book	7-28
さんじゅうさんげんどう	三十三間堂	TEMPLE	10-34
ざんねん	残念	regrettable	6-50
し	四	four	1
～じ	時	...o'clock	1-21
シカゴ		Chicago	9-21
じかん	時間	time	6-18
～じかん	～時間	...hours	5
しけん	試験	examination	15-29
しごと	仕事	work, job	4-18
じしょ	辞書	dictionary	2-02
しずか	静か	quiet	6-44
しずかに	静かに	quietly	14-36
した	下	below, under	3-29
しち	七	seven	1
しつもん	質問	question	4-19

- 124 -

しぬ	死ぬ	die	7-06
じゃ		well then	6-55
しゃしん	写真	photograph	10-12
じゅう	十	ten	1
～じゅう	～中	throughout...	5-36
～しゅうかん	～週間	...weeks	5
じゅうしょ	住所	address	8-35
しゅうまつ	週末	weekend	13-25
しゅくだい	宿題	homework	14-15
しゅみ	趣味	hobby	15-28
しょうかい	紹介	introduction	15-14
しょうがつ	正月	New Year's Day	14-19
しょうがっきん	奨学金	scholarship	12-28
しょうがっこう	小～	elem. school	15-31
じょうず	上手	skillful	12-38
しょうせつ	小説	novel	5-15
しょくじ	食事	dining	14-12
しょくどう	食堂	dining room	3-06
ジョンソン		Johnson	8-45
しらべる	調べる	check v.	14-05
しりょう	資料	material	13-15
しる	知る	know	9-09
しろい	白い	white	2-28
～じん	～人	NATIONALITY	1-14
しんじゅく	新宿	PLACE	6-25
しんぶん	新聞	newspaper	4-26
すいえい	水泳	swimming	5-10
ずいぶん	随分	very	10-43
すいようび	水曜日	Wednesday	4-36
すう	吸う	smoke	12-08
すき	好き	like, fond of	11-41
すく	空く	get uncrowded	11-05
すぐ	直ぐ	immediately	4-44
すこし	少し	a little/few	4-37
すずき	鈴木	NAME	4-35
ずっと		much more	11-44
ステーキ		steak	5-20
スポーツ		sports	5-11
スミス		Smith	1-09
すむ	住む	live, reside	8-05
する		do, play	4-16
すると		then	14-40
すわる	座る	sit	10-07
せい	背	height	9-10
せいじ	政治	politics	8-20
せいど	制度	system	13-17
せき	席	seat	10-21
せまい	狭い	narrow	9-32
せん	千	one thousand	2
せん～	先～	last...	6-51
せんせい	先生	teacher, Prof.	1-03
せんぱい	先輩	one's senior	9-17
せんもん	専門	specialty	8-18
そう		in that manner	6-30
そこ		that place	3-37
そして		and (then)	7-50
そちら		that way	7-32
そっち		=そちら	11-26
そと	外	outside	14-23
その～		that...	2-24
そば	傍	near, close	3-34
そら	空	sky	12-29
それ		that thing	2-20
それでは		well then	12-42
そんな～		that kind of	5-38

〔た〕

だい～	大～	very much	15-44
だいがく	大学	college	3-01
だいがくいん	大学院	grad. school	13-18
だいじょうぶ	大丈夫	all right	13-34
たいてい	大抵	usually	4-42
たいてい	大抵	in most cases	12-R
タイプ		typing	14-14
だいぶ	大分	quite	11-45
だいぶつ	大仏	Big Statue of Buddha	11-29
たいへん	大変	tough, hectic	6-49
たいへん	大変	very	7-41
たかい	高い	expensive, high	5-42
たかはし	高橋	NAME	14-32
たくさん	沢山	many, much	3-49
タクシー		taxi	14-29
たしか	確か	certain, sure	10-42
だす	出す	turn in, take ... out, mail	14-09
～だす	～出す	start doing...	13-09
～だす	～出す	do...out	14-10
たすかる	助かる	be saved	7-11
たずねる	訪ねる	visit	12-04
～たち	～達	...and others	3-42
たつ	立つ	stand up	7-08
たてもの	建物	building	2-15
たなか	田中	NAME	1-08
タバコ		cigarettes	12-30
たべもの	食べ物	food	15-21
たべる	食べる	eat	4-11
たまご	卵	egg	6-15
だめ	駄目	no good	9-30
たりる	足りる	be enough	6-04
だれ	誰	who	3-40
たんじょうび	誕生日	birthday	15-19
ちいさい	小さい	small	6-36
ちかい	近い	close	12-37

ちがう	違う	be different	10-04
ちかてつ	地下鉄	subway	3-13
ちず	地図	map	14-25
ちゃみせ	茶店	tea house	10-20
ちゅうがっこう	中〜	middle school	15-32
ちゅうごく	中国	China	1-05
ちょっと	一寸	a little	7-40
つかう	使う	spend	7-02
つかう	使う	use	14-R
つかれる	疲れる	get tired	12-06
つぎ	次	next	10-29
つく	着く	arrive	13-08
つくえ	机	desk	2-05
つくる	作る	make	11-08
つける	付ける	attach, put on, turn on	7-15
つつむ	包む	wrap	7-04
つとめる	務める	be employed	8-06
つまらない		uninteresting, bored	7-47
つり	釣	fishing	13-11
つる	釣る	fish v.	13-06
つれていく	連れて〜	take PEOPLE	15-01
つれてくる	連れて〜	bring PEOPLE	15-02
つれる	釣れる	be caught	13-05
て	手	hand	13-20
テープ		tape	7-25
テーブル		table	3-10
テープレコーダー		tape recorder	14-30
でかける	出掛ける	go out	5-06
てがみ	手紙	letter	10-13
テキサス		Texas	11-33
できる	出来る	be made	10-11
できる	出来る	can do	12-03
です		be, am, is	1-16
テスト		test	5-19
テニス		tennis	12-15
でも		but, however	5-45
てら	寺	Buddhist temple	10-19
でる	出る	appear	15-09
でる	出る	get out, leave	9-04
テレビ		television	4-24
てんき	天気	weather	4-20
でんしゃ	電車	train	11-15
でんわ	電話	telephone	8-15
と	戸	door	3-14
〜ど	〜度	... times	5
〜という		called...	9-02
ドイツ		Germany	8-28
どう		how (about)	6-32
とうきょう	東京	Tokyo	1-29
どうして		why	6-34
どうぞ		please	7-43
どうも		indeed, somehow	7-42
とおい	遠い	far	12-36
〜とき	〜時	when...	5-33
ときどき	時々	sometimes	4-43
とけい	時計	clock, watch	2-08
どこ		where	3-39
ところ	所	place	6-19
ところで		by the way	13-38
としょかん	図書館	library	2-17
どちら		which way	7-34
どっち		=どちら	11-28
とても		very	15-41
となり	隣り	next to	3-33
どの〜		which...	2-26
どのぐらい		to what extent	5-34
ともだち	友達	friend	6-10
どようび	土曜日	Saturday	4-36
とりにく	鳥肉	chicken meat	6-12
とる	取る	take	10-06
どれ		which one	2-22
どんな〜		what kind of	5-40

〔な〕

ない		non-existent	9-33
ナイロン		nylon	2-12
なか	中	inside, middle	3-30
ながい	長い	long	11-36
ながく	長く	for long	13-35
なかの	中野	PLACE	8-47
なかむら	中村	NAME	3-27
なつめそうせき	夏目そう石	NAME	5-28
なな	七	seven	1
なに	何	what	3-41
なら	奈良	PLACE	11-31
ならう	習う	learn	10-08
なる		become	10-05
なる	鳴る	ring v.	13-07
なん	何	what	1-31
に	二	two	1
にぎやか	賑やか	lively	6-45
にく	肉	meat	6-11
にし	西	west	11-22
〜にち	〜日	..days, DATE	5
にちようび	日曜日	Sunday	4-36
にっき	日記	diary	13-19
にほん	日本	Japan	1-07
ニューヨーク		New York	1-30
〜にん	〜人	...people	11
にんぎょう	人形	doll	15-23
ねこ	猫	cat	3-26
ねつ	熱	fever	12-24

ねむい	眠い	sleepy	13-33
ねる	寝る	go to bed, sleep	4-14
～ねん	～年	... years	5
ノート		notebook	5-23
のど	喉	throat	11-13
のみもの	飲物	drink n.	15-22
のむ	飲む	drink v.	4-10

〔は〕

は	歯	tooth	12-22
バー		bar	11-20
パーティー		party	6-07
はい		yes	2-33
～ばい	～倍	...times	11
ばいてん	売店	(news) stand	9-16
はいる	入る	enter, go into	7-13
はく	履く	wear SHOES	9-08
はこ	箱	box	3-12
はじまる	始まる	X begins	4-05
はじめ	初め	beginning	10-28
はじめる	始める	begin X	11-10
バス		bus	8-41
はち	八	eight	1
はな	花	flower	15-16
はな	鼻	nose	12-19
はなし	話	story, talk	6-06
はなす	話す	talk, speak	6-05
はなみ	花見	flower viewing	15-12
はやい	早い	early	4-49
はやい	速い	fast	4-49
はやく	早く	early adv.	6-27
はやく	速く	fast adv.	6-27
はやし	林	NAME	10-31
パリ		Paris	9-26
～(じ)はん	～時半	half past...	1-22
ばんぐみ	番組	program (TV)	5-17
ばんごう	番号	number	8-34
ひ	日	day	11-17
ピアノ		piano	13-22
ビール		beer	5-22
ひがし	東	east	11-21
ひく	引く	look up	13-R
ひく	弾く	play (instr.)	13-R
ひく	引く	pull, catch (cold)	12-05
ひくい	低い	low	9-31
ひこうき	飛行機	airplane	8-39
びじゅつ	美術	fine arts	11-18
ひと	人	person, people	3-15
ひま	暇	free time	6-43
ひゃく	百	hundred	2
びょういん	病院	hospital	2-18
びょうき	病気	illness, sick	6-17
ひる	昼	daytime, noon	1-27
ひろい	広い	wide, spacious	6-41
ふく	服	clothes	8-37
ふくしゅう	復習	review	12-12
ぶっか	物価	commodity prices	12-27
ふとる	太る	get fat	9-11
フランス		France	8-27
ふる	降る	fall (rain)	5-05
ふるい	古い	old	6-39
ぶんがく	文学	literature	8-23
ぶんぽう	文法	grammar	10-18
へいあんじんぐう	平安神宮	SHRINE	10-35
へた	下手	poor at	12-39
べつ	別	separate	10-27
へや	部屋	room	8-31
～へん	～辺	...area	13-41
ペン		pen	2-03
べんきょう	勉強	study	4-17
べんとう	弁当	boxed lunch	10-16
べんり	便利	convenient	11-40
～ほう	～方	EMPHASIS	11-12
ぼうえき	貿易	trade, trading	8-17
ほかに	外に	besides that	14-31
ほかの～	外の	other...	14-31
ぼく	僕	I (men)	10-25
ほしい	欲しい	want	15-39
ボストン		Boston	9-20
ホテル		hotel	3-07
ほん	本	book	2-01
～ほん	～本	LONG OBJECTS	5
ほんとうに	本当に	really	12-41

〔ま〕

まい～	毎	every...	4-51
～まい	～枚	THIN, FLAT OBJ	5
まえ	前	front	3-31
～まえに	～前に	...ago	10-46
まえに	前に	before	15-43
まずい	不味い	tastes awful	10-41
また	又	again	7-44
まだ		(not) yet, still	4-45
まち	町	town	11-19
まつ	待つ	wait for	7-03
まっすぐ	真っ直ぐ	straight	11-47
まつもと	松本	NAME	6-23
まど	窓	window	2-14
まんが	漫画	cartoon	15-26
みかん	蜜柑	mandarin orange	7-20

みじかい	短い	short	11-37
みず	水	water	4-22
みせ	店	shop, store	6-16
みせる	見せる	show, let see	10-10
みち	道	road	14-24
みちこ	道子	NAME	7-35
みなさん	皆さん	all, everyone	10-36
みなみ	南	south	11-23
みみ	耳	ear	12-20
ミラー		Miller	9-19
みる	見る	look at, see	4-12
～てみる		do...and see	13-10
みんな	皆	all, everyone	10-36
むずかしい	難しい	difficult	11-34
め	目	eye	12-18
めいし	名刺	business card	8-33
めがね	眼鏡	glasses	9-13
メロン		melon	7-21
もう～		...more	9-34
もう		already, (not) any more	4-46
もうすぐ		soon	13-36
もくようび	木曜日	Thursday	4-36
もしもし		hello PHONE	8-54
モスクワ		Moscow	9-25
もつ	持つ	hold, have	8-07
もっていく	持って～	take THINGS	15-03
もってくる	持って～	bring THINGS	15-04
もっと		more	11-43
もどる	戻る	return	14-06
もの	物	thing, object	6-20
もめん	木綿	cotton	2-13
もらう		receive	10-09
もり	森	NAME	6-24
もりたよしこ	森田良子	NAME	15-35

〔や〕

～や	～屋	store, shop	6-54
やきゅう	野球	baseball	5-09
やくしょ	役所	gov't office	8-32
やくにたつ	役に立つ	be helpful	7-09
やさい	野菜	vegetable	6-13
やさしい	易しい	easy	11-35
やすい	安い	inexpensive	6-37
やすみ	休み	vacation	4-33
やすみ	休み	closed	12-R
やすむ	休む	be absent, rest	14-07
やせる	痩せる	get thin	9-10
やまぐち	山口	NAME	7-36
やました	山下	NAME	4-34
やまもと	山本	NAME	6-21
やめる	辞める	quit	11-09
やる		do, play	5-07
ゆうがた	夕方	early evening	5-32
ゆうびんきょく	郵便局	post office	3-03
ゆうべ	夕	last night	10-37
ゆき	雪	snow	5-13
ゆっくり		slowly	7-45
よう	用	errand	9-15
ようじ	用事	errand	13-12
～ようび	曜日	DAYS OF WEEK	4-36
ヨーロッパ		Europe	15-34
よく		often, a lot	5-43
よく		well	10-45
よこ	横	side, beside	3-35
よしかわ	吉川	NAME	5-27
よしだ	吉田	NAME	5-25
よしむら	吉村	NAME	11-30
よしゅう	予習	preparation	12-11
よてい	予定	plan, schedule	13-13
よぶ	呼ぶ	call, invite	7-05
よむ	読む	read	4-09
よる	夜	night	1-28
よん	四	four	1

〔ら〕

らい～	来～	next...	6-53
らいねん	来年	next year	13-28
ラジオ		radio	7-24
ラボ		language lab.	7-26
～り		...people	11
りっぱ	立派	stately	6-47
リボン		ribbon	7-23
りょう	寮	dormitory	4-29
りょうしん	両親	parents	12-26
りんご		apple	7-19
れい	零	zero	8-42
れきし	歴史	history	8-24
レコード		record	5-24
ろく	六	six	1
ロサンゼルス		Los Angeles	9-22
ロシア		Russia	8-29
ロビー		lobby	3-08
ロンドン		London	9-24
ろんぶん	論文	dissertation	13-14

〔わ〕

わかい	若い	young	8-53
わかる	分かる	understand	4-04
ワシントン		Washington	9-23
わたし	私	I	1-01

English-Japanese Glossary

ENGLISH	JAPANESE	KANJI	LESS. NO.-WORD NO.
	[A]		
a.m.	ごぜん	午前	1-23
about...	〜ぐらい		5-35
above	うえ	上	3-28
be absent	やすむ	休む	14-07
address	じゅうしょ	住所	8-35
after...	〜あと	〜後	4-41
afternoon	ごご	午後	1-24
again	また	又	7-44
...ago	〜まえ	〜前	10-46
airmail	こうくうびん	航空便	15-27
airplane	ひこうき	飛行機	8-39
all right	だいじょうぶ	大丈夫	13-34
all, everyone	みんな	皆	10-36
already	もう		4-46
America	アメリカ		1-04
and then	そして		7-50
...and others	〜たち	〜達	3-42
answer v.	こたえる	答える	7-18
answer n.	こたえ	答	14-28
(not) any more	もう		4-46
apartment	アパート		6-08
appear	でる	出る	15-09
apple	りんご		7-19
... area	〜へん	〜辺	13-41
around...	〜ごろ	〜頃	4-53
arrive	つく	着く	13-08
ask	きく	聞く	7-01
at a loss	こまる	困る	12-07
attach	つける	付ける	7-15
	[B]		
back of	うしろ	後ろ	3-32
bag	かばん	鞄	2-09
bank	ぎんこう	銀行	3-04
bar	バー		11-20
baseball	やきゅう	野球	5-09
be, am, is	です		1-16
be (POLITE)	いらっしゃる		15-05
become	なる		10-05
beer	ビール		5-22
before	まえに	前に	15-43
begin X	はじめる	始める	11-10
X begins	はじまる	始まる	4-05
beginning	はじめ	初め	10-28
behind	うしろ	後ろ	3-32
below	した	下	3-29
beside	よこ	横	3-35
besides that	ほかに	外に	14-31
big	おおきい	大きい	6-35
big	おおきな〜	大きな〜	14-35
BIG BUILDINGS	〜かん	〜館	11-48
birthday	たんじょうび	誕生日	15-19
bite	かむ	嚙む	12-09
black	くろい	黒い	2-29
blue	あおい	青い	2-30
book	ほん	本	2-01
bored, boring	つまらない		7-47
borrow	かりる	借りる	14-03
Boston	ボストン		9-20
bottom	した	下	3-29
box	はこ	箱	3-12
boxed lunch	べんとう	弁当	10-16
boy	おとこのこ	男の子	3-19
briefcase	かばん	鞄	2-09
bright	あかるい	明るい	10-38
bring PEOPLE	つれてくる	連れて〜	15-02
bring THINGS	もってくる	持って〜	15-04
building	たてもの	建物	2-15
bus	バス		8-41
business card	めいし	名刺	8-33
bustling	にぎやか	賑やか	6-45
busy	いそがしい	忙しい	6-42
but, however	でも		5-45
buy	かう	買う	5-08
by the way	ところで		13-38
	[C]		
called...	〜という		9-02
call	よぶ	呼ぶ	7-05
call (phone)	かける	掛ける	8-14
camera	カメラ		15-33
can do	できる	出来る	12-03
car	くるま	車	8-40
cartoon	まんが	漫画	15-26
cat	ねこ	猫	3-26
catch (cold)	ひく	引く	12-05
catch (fish)	つる	釣る	13-06
(fish) be caught	つれる	釣れる	13-05
certain	たしか	確か	10-42
chair, stool	いす	椅子	2-06
cheap	やすい	安い	6-37
check v.	しらべる	調べる	14-05

English	kana	kanji	ref
Chicago	シカゴ		9-21
chicken meat	とりにく	鳥肉	6-12
church	きょうかい	教会	4-32
cigarettes	タバコ		12-30
class	クラス		10-26
classroom	きょうしつ	教室	3-02
clean	きれい		6-46
clock	とけい	時計	2-08
close	そば	傍	3-34
close	ちかい	近い	12-37
closed	やすみ	休み	12-R
clothes	ふく	服	8-37
coffee shop	きっさてん	喫茶店	3-05
coffee	コーヒー		3-11
cold n.	かぜ	風邪	12-23
cold a.	さむい	寒い	11-39
collect	あつめる	集める	13-04
college	だいがく	大学	3-01
come	くる	来る	4-15
come (POLITE)	いらっしゃる		15-05
come doing...	～てくる	～て来る	12-10
commodity price	ぶっか	物価	12-27
company	かいしゃ	会社	4-30
concert	おんがくかい	音楽会	15-25
convenient	べんり	便利	11-40
cooked rice	ごはん	御飯	4-21
cotton	もめん	木綿	2-13
country	くに	国	12-25
(get) crowded	こむ	込む	11-06
customer	きゃく	客	8-30
cute	かわいい	可愛い	15-38

〔D〕

English	kana	kanji	ref
dark	くらい	暗い	10-39
day after tomor.	あさって	明後日	14-34
day before yest.	おととい	一昨日	5-31
day	ひ	日	11-17
DAYS OF WEEK	～ようび	～曜日	4-36
daytime	ひる	昼	1-27
be decided	きまる	決まる	15-06
delicious	おいしい		6-40
desk	つくえ	机	2-05
diary	にっき	日記	13-19
dictionary	じしょ	辞書	2-02
die	しぬ	死ぬ	7-06
differ	ちがう	違う	10-04
different...	べつの～	別の～	10-27
difficult	むずかしい	難しい	11-34
dining room	しょくどう	食堂	3-06
dining	しょくじ	食事	14-12
direction	みち	道	14-24
directly	まっすぐ	真っ直ぐ	11-47

English	kana	kanji	ref
disgusting	いや	嫌	4-48
child	こども	子供	3-16
China	ちゅうごく	中国	1-05
dislike	きらい	嫌い	15-40
dissertation	ろんぶん	論文	13-14
do... and see	～てみる		13-10
do... out	～だす	出す	14-10
doctor	いしゃ	医者	14-20
dog	いぬ	犬	3-25
doll	にんぎょう	人形	15-23
door	と	戸	3-14
dormitory	りょう	寮	4-29
do	する		4-16
do	やる		5-07
drink n.	のみもの	飲物	15-22
drink v.	のむ	飲む	4-10
(get) dry	かわく	渇く	11-04

〔E〕

English	kana	kanji	ref
ear	みみ	耳	12-20
early adj.	はやい	早い	4-49
early adv.	はやく	早く	6-27
early evening	ゆうがた	夕方	5-32
east	ひがし	東	11-21
easy	やさしい	易しい	11-35
eat	たべる	食べる	4-11
economy	けいざい	経済	8-19
egg	たまご	卵	6-15
eight	はち	八	1
elevator	エレベーター		3-09
elem. school	しょうがっこう	小～	15-31
be employed	つとめる	務める	8-06
... employee	～いん	～員	14-37
employment	こよう	雇用	13-17
end	おわる	終わる	4-06
end	さいご	最後	10-30
end of term	きまつ	期末	15-30
energetic	げんき	元気	6-48
England	イギリス		8-26
English lang.	えいご	英語	8-25
be enough	たりる	足りる	6-04
enter	あがる	上がる	7-12
enter	はいる	入る	7-13
enterprise	きぎょう	企業	13-16
errand	ようじ	用事	13-12
errand	よう	用	9-15
Europe	ヨーロッパ		15-34
every...	まい～	毎	4-51
everyone	みんな	皆	10-36
examination	しけん	試験	15-29
exercise	うんどう	運動	14-16
exist	ある	有る	3-43

English	Kana	Kanji	Ref
exist	いる	居る	3-44
expensive	たかい	高い	6-49
experience	けいけん	経験	12-13
eye	め	目	12-18

〔F〕

English	Kana	Kanji	Ref
face	かお	顔	9-14
fall (rain)	ふる	降る	5-05
far	とおい	遠い	12-36
fast adv.	はやく	速く	6-27
fast adj.	はやい	速い	4-49
(get) fat	ふとる	太る	9-11
feast	ごちそう	御馳走	15-15
female	おんな	女	3-20
fever	ねつ	熱	12-24
a few	ちょっと	一寸	7-04
a few	すこし	少し	4-03
fine arts	びじゅつ	美術	11-18
finish	おわる	終わる	4-06
first	はじめ	初め	10-28
fish n.	さかな	魚	6-14
fishing	つり	釣	13-11
five	ご	五	1
flower	はな	花	15-16
flower viewing	はなみ	花見	15-12
food	たべもの	食べ物	15-21
foot	あし	足	13-21
for long	ながく	長く	13-35
four	よん, し	四	1
France	フランス		8-27
free time	ひま	暇	6-43
fresh	あたらしい	新しい	6-38
Friday	きんようび	金曜日	4-36
friend	ともだち	友達	6-10
from now on	これから		11-46
front	まえ	前	3-31
fruit	くだもの	果物	7-22

〔G〕

English	Kana	Kanji	Ref
Gee...	さあ		8-55
Germany	ドイツ		8-28
get out	でる	出る	9-04
get up	おきる	起きる	4-13
Ginza	ぎんざ	銀座	8-46
girl	おんなのこ	女の子	3-22
give	あげる	上げる	7-16
give	さしあげる	差し〜	7-17
glad	うれしい	嬉しい	13-32
glasses	めがね	眼鏡	9-13
go back	かえる	帰る	4-07
go into	はいる	入る	7-13
go out	でかける	出掛ける	5-06
go to bed	ねる	寝る	4-14
go up to/on	あがる	上がる	7-12
good	いい	良い	4-47
gov't office	やくしょ	役所	8-32
go	いく	行く	4-08
go (POLITE)	いらっしゃる		15-05
grad. school	だいがくいん	大学院	13-18
grammar	ぶんぽう	文法	10-18
grandfather	おじいさん		10-23
grandmother	おばあさん		10-24
guest	きゃく	客	8-30
guide	あんない	案内	15-11
guitar	ギター		13-23
gum	ガム		12-31

〔H〕

English	Kana	Kanji	Ref
hair	かみ(のけ)	髪の毛	12-17
half past...	〜じはん	〜時半	1-22
hand	て	手	13-20
handy	べんり	便利	11-40
have, own	もっている	持って〜	8-07
Hayashi	はやし	林	10-31
head	あたま	頭	12-16
healthy	げんき	元気	6-48
heart	こころ	心	5-29
hear	きく	聞く	7-01
Heian Shrine	へいあんじんぐう	平安神宮	10-35
height	せい	背	9-12
hello PHONE	もしもし		8-54
be helpful	やくにたつ	役に立つ	7-09
here	ここ		3-36
he	かれ	彼	12-33
high school	こうこう	高校	5-16
high	たかい	高い	5-24
history	れきし	歴史	8-24
hobby	しゅみ	趣味	15-28
hold	もつ	持つ	8-07
holiday	やすみ	休み	4-33
homework	しゅくだい	宿題	14-15
home	うち	家	4-28
hospital	びょういん	病院	2-18
hot	あつい	暑い	11-38
hotel	ホテル		3-07
house	うち	家	4-28
house POLITE	おたく	お宅	7-29
how (about)	いかが		6-33
how (about)	どう		6-32
how many, etc.	どのぐらい		5-34
how many	いくつ	幾つ	7-39
how much (money)	いくら	幾ら	2-31

English	かな	漢字	Ref
how old	いくつ		15-36
however	けれども		13-39
however	でも		5-45
hundred	ひゃく	百	1
hurry	いそぐ	急ぐ	7-07
husband	(ご)しゅじん	主人	3-23

〔 I 〕

English	かな	漢字	Ref
I 〔MALE〕	ぼく	僕	10-25
I	わたし	私	1-01
ice cream	アイスクリーム		12-32
illness	びょうき	病気	6-17
immediately	すぐ	直ぐ	4-44
impressive	りっぱ	立派	6-47
in most cases	たいてい	大抵	12-R
indeed	どうも		7-42
inexpensive	やすい	安い	6-37
inside	なか	中	3-30
interesting	おもしろい	面白い	7-46
introduction	しょうかい	紹介	15-14
invite	よぶ	呼ぶ	7-05
Ito	いとう	伊藤	13-24

〔 J 〕

English	かな	漢字	Ref
Japan	にほん	日本	1-07
job	しごと	仕事	4-18
Johnson	ジョンソン		8-45
(one's) junior	こうはい	後輩	9-18

〔 K 〕

English	かな	漢字	Ref
Kamakura	かまくら	鎌倉	11-32
Kawakami	かわかみ	川上	8-44
Kiyomizu Temple	きよみずでら	清水寺	10-33
know	しる	知る	9-09
Kobayashi	こばやし	小林	6-22
Korea	かんこく	韓国	1-06
Kyoto	きょうと	京都	10-32

〔 L 〕

English	かな	漢字	Ref
language lab.	ラボ		7-26
language	ことば	言葉	10-17
... language	～ご	～語	1-15
large	おおきい	大きい	6-35
last night	ゆうべ	夕	10-37
last year	きょねん	去年	8-49
last...	せん～	先～	6-51
(the) last	さいご	最後	10-30
later	あとで	後で	8-51
late adv.	おそく	遅く	6-28
late adj.	おそい	遅い	4-50
learn	ならう	習う	10-08
leave	でる	出る	9-04
lend	かす	貸す	14-04
lending service	かしだし	貸し出し	14-11
let see	みせる	見せる	10-10
letter	てがみ	手紙	10-13
library	としょかん	図書館	2-17
light	あかるい	明るい	10-38
like	すき	好き	11-41
liquor	さけ	酒	14-22
a little	すこし	少し	4-03
a little	ちょっと	一寸	7-04
lively	にぎやか	賑やか	6-45
live, reside	すむ	住む	8-05
lobby	ロビー		3-08
London	ロンドン		9-24
long	ながい	長い	11-36
look for	さがす	探す	11-07
look up	ひく	引く	13-R
look	みる	見る	4-12
Los Angeles	ロサンゼルス		9-22
low	ひくい	低い	9-31

〔 M 〕

English	かな	漢字	Ref
machine	きかい	機械	8-38
be made	できる	出来る	10-11
magazine	ざっし	雑誌	4-27
mail v.	だす	出す	14-09
make	つくる	作る	11-08
male	おとこ	男	3-17
man	おとこのひと	男の人	3-18
mandarin orange	みかん	蜜柑	7-20
many	たくさん	沢山	3-49
map	ちず	地図	14-25
marriage	けっこん	結婚	8-16
material	しりょう	資料	13-15
Matsumoto	まつもと	松本	6-23
meal	ごはん	御飯	4-21
meat	にく	肉	6-11
med. science	いがく	医学	8-22
medicine	くすり	薬	14-21
meeting place	かいじょう	会場	6-09
meeting	かいぎ	会議	14-13
meeting	かいぎ	会議	14-13
meet	あう	会う	6-03
melon	メロン		7-21
Michiko	みちこ	道子	7-35
middle school	ちゅうがっこう	中～	15-32
middle	なか	中	3-30
Miller	ミラー		9-19
mind v.	かまう	構う	11-11

English	Kana	Kanji	Ref
Monday	げつようび	月曜日	4-36
money	おかね	お金	8-36
...month	〜げつ	〜月	7-49
...more	もう〜		9-34
more	もっと		11-43
Mori	もり	森	6-24
morning	あさ	朝	1-26
Moscow	モスクワ		9-25
most, the most	いちばん	一番	15-42
mouth	くち	口	12-21
movie	えいが	映画	4-25
Mr., Ms.	さん		1-12
Mr., Ms.	せんせい	先生	1-13
much more	ずっと		11-44
much	たくさん	沢山	3-49
(not) much	あまり		5-44
music	おんがく	音楽	10-14

[N]

English	Kana	Kanji	Ref
Nakamura	なかむら	中村	3-27
Nakano	なかの	中野	8-47
named	という		9-02
Nara	なら	奈良	11-31
narrow	せまい	狭い	9-32
near	そば	傍	3-34
...ness	〜さ		11-49
New Year's Day	しょうがつ	正月	14-19
New York	ニューヨーク		1-30
new	あたらしい	新しい	6-38
newspaper	しんぶん	新聞	4-26
next to	となり	隣り	3-33
next year	らいねん	来年	13-28
next...	らい〜	来〜	6-53
next	つぎ	次	10-29
nice	いい	良い	4-47
night	よる	夜	1-28
nine	きゅう, く	九	1
no good	だめ	駄目	9-30
noisy	うるさい		10-40
non-existent	ない		9-33
noon	ひる	昼	1-27
north	きた	北	11-24
nose	はな	鼻	12-19
notebook	ノート		5-23
novel	しょうせつ	小説	5-15
now	いま	今	1-25
no	いいえ		1-11
number	ばんごう	番号	8-34
number	かず	数	11-16
nylon	ナイロン		2-12

[O]

English	Kana	Kanji	Ref
...o'clock	〜じ	〜時	
(not) often	あまり		5-44
often, a lot	よく		5-43
oh	ああ		2-34
old man	おじいさん		10-23
old woman	おばあさん		10-24
old	ふるい	古い	6-39
one	いち	一	1
on (top of)	うえ	上	3-28
or less	いない	以内	14-38
or thereafter	〜いご	以後	14-39
other...	ほかの〜	外の	14-31
outside	そと	外	14-23
over there	あそこ		3-38

[P]

English	Kana	Kanji	Ref
p.m.	ごご	午後	1-24
painful	いたい	痛い	12-35
paper	かみ	紙	5-14
pardon?	え(っ)		12-44
parents	りょうしん	両親	12-26
Paris	パリ		9-26
park	こうえん	公園	7-30
part-time job	アルバイト		12-14
party	パーティー		6-07
pen	ペン		2-03
pencil	えんぴつ	鉛筆	2-04
people, person	ひと	人	3-15
...people	〜り/にん	〜人	11
period	きかん	期間	14-17
person	ひと	人	3-15
photograph	しゃしん	写真	10-12
piano	ピアノ		13-22
place	ところ	所	6-19
plan	よてい	予定	13-13
play	あそぶ	遊ぶ	8-11
play (instr.)	ひく	弾く	13-R
play (sports)	する		4-R
play (sports)	やる		5-07
please	どうぞ		7-43
politics	せいじ	政治	8-20
poor at	へた	下手	12-39
post office	ゆうびんきょく	郵便局	3-03
pour into	いれる	入れる	7-14
preparation	よしゅう	予習	12-11
present	おくりもの	贈り物	15-20
pretty	きれい	綺麗	6-46
program (TV)	ばんぐみ	番組	5-17
pull	ひく	引く	12-05

English	kana	kanji	ref
put into	いれる	入れる	7-14
put on, attach	つける	付ける	7-15
put on, wear	きる	着る	8-08

〔Q〕

English	kana	kanji	ref
question	しつもん	質問	4-19
quiet	しずか	静か	6-44
quietly	しずかに	静かに	14-36
quite	だいぶ	大分	11-45
quit	やめる	辞める	11-09

〔R〕

English	kana	kanji	ref
radio	ラジオ		7-24
rain	あめ	雨	5-12
read	よむ	読む	4-09
really	ほんとうに	本当に	12-41
receive	もらう		10-09
recently	このごろ	この頃	6-26
recently	このあいだ	この間	9-28
record	レコード		5-24
red	あかい	赤い	2-27
reference book	さんこうしょ	参考書	7-28
regrettable	ざんねん	残念	6-50
research	けんきゅう	研究	15-13
rest	やすむ	休む	14-07
return	もどる	戻る	14-06
return	かえる	帰る	4-07
review	ふくしゅう	復習	12-12
ribbon	リボン		7-23
right away	すぐ	直ぐ	4-44
ring v.	なる	鳴る	13-07
road	みち	道	14-24
room	へや	部屋	8-31
...room	～しつ	室	15-13
rough, tough	たいへん	大変	6-49
rule	きそく	規則	14-26
Russia	ロシア		8-29

〔S〕

English	kana	kanji	ref
Saito	さいとう	斉藤	7-37
salad	サラダ		5-21
same	おなじ	同じ	11-42
Sanjusangendo	さんじゅうさんげんどう	三十三間堂	10-34
Sato	さとう	佐藤	5-26
Saturday	どようび	土曜日	4-36
be saved	たすかる	助かる	7-11
say	いう	言う	9-05
scholarship	しょうがっきん	奨学金	12-28
school term	がっき	学期	14-18
school	がっこう	学校	2-16
science	かがく	科学	8-21
seat	せき	席	10-21
see	みる	見る	4-12
see (person)	あう	会う	6-03
sell	うる	売る	8-12
send	おくる	送る	15-08
(one's) senior	せんぱい	先輩	9-17
separate	べつ	別	10-27
seven	しち,なな	七	1
she	かのじょ	彼女	12-34
Shinjuku	しんじゅく	新宿	6-25
shoes	くつ	靴	2-10
shopping	かいもの	買物	15-10
shop	みせ	店	6-16
shop	～や	～屋	6-54
short time ago	さっき		8-50
short	みじかい	短い	11-37
show v.	みせる	見せる	10-10
sick	びょうき	病気	6-17
side	よこ	横	3-35
sing	うたう	歌う	15-07
sit	すわる	座る	10-07
six	ろく	六	1
skillful	じょうず	上手	12-38
sky	そら	空	12-29
sleep	ねる	寝る	4-14
sleepy	ねむい	眠い	13-33
slowly	ゆっくり		7-45
small	ちいさい	小さい	6-36
small (change)	こまかい	細かい	8-52
Smith	スミス		1-09
smoke v.	すう	吸う	12-08
snow	ゆき	雪	5-13
socks	くつした	靴下	2-11
somehow	どうも		7-42
sometimes	ときどき	時々	4-43
song	うた	歌	15-24
soon	もうすぐ		13-36
south	みなみ	南	11-23
spacious	ひろい	広い	6-41
speak	はなす	話す	6-05
specialty	せんもん	専門	8-18
spend	つかう	使う	14-R
sports	スポーツ		5-11
stand up	たつ	立つ	7-08
(news) stand	ばいてん	売店	9-16
start X	はじめる	始める	11-10
X starts	はじまる	始まる	4-05
start doing...	～だす	～出す	13-09
station	えき	駅	4-31
Statue of Buddha	だいぶつ	大仏	11-29

English	Kana	Kanji	Ref
stay	いる	居る	4-R
steak	ステーキ		5-20
still	まだ		4-45
stomach	おなか		11-14
store	みせ	店	6-16
story	はなし	話	6-06
student	がくせい	学生	1-02
study	べんきょう	勉強	4-17
subway	ちかてつ	地下鉄	3-13
suddenly	きゅうに	急に	12-40
Sunday	にちようび	日曜日	4-36
sure	たしか	確か	10-42
Suzuki	すずき	鈴木	4-35
sweets, snack	おかし	お菓子	10-15
swimming	すいえい	水泳	5-10
system	せいど	制度	13-17

〔T〕

English	Kana	Kanji	Ref
table	テーブル		3-10
Takahashi	たかはし	高橋	14-32
take...along	つれていく	連れて〜	15-01
take...along	もっていく	持って〜	15-03
take..out	だす	出す	14-09
take	とる	取る	10-06
talk v.	はなす	話す	6-05
talk	はなし	話	6-06
Tanaka	たなか	田中	1-08
tape recorder	テープレコーダー		14-30
tape	テープ		7-25
taste awful	まずい	不味い	10-41
taxi	タクシー		14-29
tea house	ちゃみせ	茶店	10-20
tea	おちゃ	お茶	4-23
teach	おしえる	教える	8-13
teacher	せんせい	先生	1-03
telephone	でんわ	電話	8-15
television	テレビ		4-24
tell	おしえる	教える	8-13
(Buddhist) temple	てら	寺	10-19
ten	じゅう	十	1
tennis	テニス		12-15
test	テスト		5-19
Texas	テキサス		11-33
that direction	あちら		7-33
that direction	そちら		7-32
that kind of	あんな〜		5-39
that kind of	そんな〜		5-38
that place	そこ		3-37
that place	あそこ		3-38
that thing	それ		2-20
that thing	あれ		2-21
that way	ああ		6-31
that way	そう		6-30
that...	その		2-24
that...	あの		2-25
(and) then	そして		7-50
then, thereupon	すると		14-40
there is/are	いる		3-45
there is/are	ある		3-43
there	そこ		3-37
thesis	ろんぶん	論文	13-14
(get) thin	やせる	痩せる	9-10
thing	もの	物	6-20
thing, event	こと	事	5-18
think	おもう	思う	9-06
this direction	こちら		7-31
this kind of	こんな		5-37
this manner	こう		6-29
this morning	けさ	今朝	9-27
this person	こちら〔POLITE〕		8-43
this place	ここ		3-36
this thing	これ		2-19
this year	ことし	今年	13-27
this...	この〜		2-23
this/next time	こんど	今度	8-48
this...	こん〜	今〜	6-52
thousand	せん	千	2-51
three	さん	三	1
throat	のど	喉	11-13
throughout	〜じゅう	〜中	5-36
Thursday	もくようび	木曜日	4-36
ticket	きっぷ	切符	7-27
...times	〜ばい	〜倍	11
time	じかん	時間	6-18
(get) tired	つかれる	疲れる	12-06
today	きょう	今日	4-38
together	いっしょに	一緒に	13-37
Tokyo	とうきょう	東京	1-29
tomorrow	あした	明日	4-39
tonight	こんばん	今晩	4-40
tooth	は	歯	12-22
top	うえ	上	3-28
tough, hectic	たいへん	大変	6-49
town	まち	町	11-19
trade, trading	ぼうえき	貿易	8-17
train	でんしゃ	電車	11-15
try one's best	がんばる	頑張る	7-10
Tuesday	かようび	火曜日	4-36
turn in	だす	出す	14-09
turn on	つける	付ける	7-15
two	に	二	1
typewriter	タイプ		14-14

[U]

um...	あの（う）		12-43
umbrella	かさ	傘	2-07
(get) uncrowded	すく	空く	11-05
under	した	下	3-29
understand	わかる	分かる	4-04
uninteresting	つまらない		7-47
unpleasant	いや	嫌	4-48
use	つかう	使う	7-02
usually	たいてい	大抵	4-42

[V]

vacation	やすみ	休み	4-33
various	いろいろ	色々	5-41
variously	いろいろ	色々	10-44
vegetable	やさい	野菜	6-13
very much	だい〜	大〜	15-44
very	ずいぶん	随分	10-43
very	とても		15-41
very	たいへん	大変	7-41
(not) very	あまり		5-44
visit	たずねる	訪ねる	12-04
voice	こえ	声	14-27

[W]

wait	まつ	待つ	7-03
wake... up	おこす	起こす	14-08
walk	あるく	歩く	8-10
wallet	さいふ	財布	10-22
want	ほしい	欲しい	15-39
Washington	ワシントン		9-20
watch v.	みる	見る	4-12
watch n.	とけい	時計	2-08
water	みず	水	4-22
wear (clothes)	きる	着る	8-08
wear (glasses)	かける	掛ける	9-07
wear (shoes)	はく	履く	9-08
weather	てんき	天気	4-20
Wednesday	すいようび	水曜日	4-36
week after next	さらいしゅう	再来週	13-26
weekend	しゅうまつ	週末	13-25
well adj.	げんき	元気	6-48
well adv.	よく		10-45
well then	じゃ		6-55
well then	それでは		12-42
Well gee...	さあ		8-55
west	にし	西	11-22
what extent	どのぐらい		5-34
what kind of	どんな〜		5-40
what	なに	何	3-41
what	なん	何	1-31
when	いつ〔QW〕		7-38
when...	〜とき	〜時	5-33
where	どこ		3-39
which one	どれ (of 3 or more)		2-22
which one	どちら (of 2)		11-28
which way	どちら		7-34
which...	どの〜		2-26
while...	〜あいだ	〜間	13-31
white	しろい	白い	2-28
who	だれ	誰	3-40
why	どうして		6-34
wide	ひろい	広い	6-41
wife〔POLITE〕	おくさん	奥さん	3-24
window	まど	窓	2-14
woman	おんなのひと	女の人	3-21
word, phrase	ことば	言葉	10-17
work	しごと	仕事	4-18
wrap	つつむ	包む	7-04
write	かく	書く	8-09

[Y]

Yamaguchi	やまぐち	山口	7-36
Yamamoto	やまもと	山本	6-21
Yamashita	やました	山下	4-34
yeah	うん		13-40
year after next	さらいねん	再来年	13-29
year before last	おととし	一昨年	13-30
...years old	〜さい	歳	15-37
...yen	〜えん	〜円	2-32
yes	ええ		1-10
yes	はい		2-33
yesterday	きのう	昨日	5-30
(not) yet	まだ		4-45
Yoshida	よしだ	吉田	5-25
Yoshikawa	よしかわ	吉川	5-27
Yoshiko Morita	もりたよしこ	森田良子	15-35
Yoshimura	よしむら	吉村	11-30
you〔MALE〕	きみ	君	14-33
young	わかい	若い	8-53
younger brother	おとうと	弟	15-17
younger sister	いもうと	妹	15-18

[Z]

zero	れい, ゼロ	零	8-42

INDEX TO THE GRAMMATICAL PATTERNS

A wa B ga C -- 79, 86
action in progress -- 57
adverbial form -- 71
adverbs -- 26
aida-clause -- 99
amari -- 32
amount expressions -- 33
ba form -- 105
ba ii n desu -- 105
choice questions -- 42
comparison construction -- 79
conjunctive particles -- 15, 120
copula -- 39, 63, 71, 72
daroo -- 81
-dasu -- 91, 100
de P. "within" -- 91, 118
de P. [MEANS] -- 58, 83, 118
de P. [PLACE] -- 24, 118
deshoo(ka) -- 50, 65
dictionary form -- 23
e P. [DIRECTION] -- 24, 118
existence construction -- 17
ga P. "but" -- 41, 120
ga P. [OBJECT] -- 83, 112, 113, 117
ga P. [SUBJECT] -- 15, 98, 107, 117
-garu -- 112
go- (prefix) -- 60, 116
grammatical particles -- 15, 117
hanasu -- 43
hazu desu -- 106
hoo -- 79, 81
hoshii, hoshi-gatte-iru -- 111
i-type adjectives -- 11, 39, 63, 71
irassharu -- 113
ka P. "or" -- 91, 119
ka P. [QUESTION] -- 4, 120
ka mo shiremasen -- 90
kara P. "from" -- 68, 119
kara P. "so" -- 51, 82, 115, 120
keredomo P. "but" -- 97, 120
ko-so-a-do words -- 9, 35
kudasai, -te kudasai -- 11, 48, 86
locational nouns -- 18

mada -- 67
made P. "until" -- 68, 107, 119
made ni P. [DEADLINE] -- 107, 119
mashita -- 32, 90
mashoo(ka) -- 49
mo ...mo P. "both" -- 76, 119
mo [SIMILARITY] -- 12, 15, 27, 60, 119
moo -- 67
motto -- 80
n(o) desu -- 86, 104
na-type adjectives -- 39, 63, 71, 72
nagara -- 89
nai -- 106
ne(e) P. [AMAZEMENT] -- 28, 120
ne P. [TAG QUESTION] -- 15, 120
negative questions -- 41
ni P. "per" -- 33, 118
ni P. [DESTINATION] -- 53, 118
ni P. [PLACE] -- 17, 59, 117
ni P. [PURPOSE] -- 58, 117
ni P. [SOURCE] -- 107, 117
ni P. [TARGET] -- 43, 117
ni P. [TIME] -- 24, 32, 118
ni tsuite "about" -- 91, 120
no (clause no) -- 89
no P. [NOUN MODIFICATION] -- 16, 118
no P. [SUBJECT] -- 68, 118
no de P. "so" -- 59, 82, 115, 120
noun modification -- 16, 66, 73
o- (prefix) -- 60, 116
o P. [OBJECT] -- 11, 117
o P. [PLACE OF MOTION] -- 61, 117
particles -- 15, 117
permission -- 103
plain form -- 63, 71, 81
polite expressions -- 115
prefixes -- 60, 116
prohibition -- 103
purpose construction -- 58
question marks -- 43
quotation -- 65
QW de mo -- 51
QW ka -- 34

QW mo -- 34
reason clauses -- 51, 59, 82, 98
relative clause -- 73
request -- 11, 48, 86
resultant state -- 57, 90
semantic particles -- 15, 120
sentence particles -- 15, 120
soo "seem" -- 94
stem -- 39, 116
suggestion -- 50
suki(na) -- 79, 86, 111
sukoshi -- 52
supposition -- 50
taihen -- 52
-te form -- 40, 48, 49, 86, 90, 91, 98
-te iru -- 57, 90
-te kuru -- 83
-te miru -- 91
-te mo ii desu -- 103
-te wa ikemasen -- 103
tense -- 23, 32, 99, 104
time expressions -- 32
to P. "and" -- 28, 119
to P. "with" -- 58, 119

to P. [QUOTATION] -- 81, 120
to iu PPhr "called" -- 61, 120
toki-clause -- 99, 104
tsumori desu -- 114
V (past) koto ga arimasu -- 114
V (stem)-nagara -- 89
V (stem)-soo -- 95
V (stem)-tai desu -- 113
V-ta/-nai hoo ga ii desu -- 81
V (vol.) to omotte imasu -- 96
V (vol.) to shita toki -- 97
verbal nouns -- 26
verbs -- 23, 32, 63, 72
volitional form -- 96
wa P. [TOPIC, CONTRAST] -- 4, 11, 15, 27, 98, 107, 119
wh-questions -- 25, 88
word order -- 25
X wa QW desu ka -- 4, 10
X wa Y desu (ka) -- 4, 19
ya P. "and so forth" -- 76, 119
yo P. [EMPHASIS] -- 28, 120
yoku -- 32
yori P. "than" -- 76, 119
yotee desu -- 96